My Life Story

My Life Story

MARCIA NICKS

ARPress
ILLUMINATING IDEAS
EMPOWERING VOICES

ARPress
45 Dan Road Suite 5
Canton MA 02021

Hotline: 1(888) 821-0229
Fax: 1(508) 545-7580

Ordering Information:
Quantity sales. Special discounts are available on quantity purchases by corporations, associations, and others. For details, contact the publisher at the address above.

Printed in the United States of America.
ISBN-13:   Paperback   979-8-89356-811-0
              eBook   979-8-89356-812-7

Library of Congress Control Number: 2024904712

Table of Contents

MY JOURNEY

My purpose for writing this book is to encourage others. No matter how dark life seems, our Father in Heaven and maker has given you the strength to make it through. For "...God's strength is made perfect in weakness 2 Corinthians 12:9"

Acknowledgements

My utmost gratitude is to my Lord and Savior, Jesus Christ. I am grateful for the wisdom that he has given me to complete this book.

I would like to Thank my late husband, Comadore Nicks, for patiently listening to me explaining why I should write this book. His final advice was," sugar, if you feel this way, I suggest you write the book.

I would like to thank Angela Wynn for inspiring me to stop procrastinating an complete the book, Stating,"you don't have as much time as you think".

I would like to thank my daughter, Mary Woods, for proofreading and correcting errors in the material. I would like to thank her for helping me to get the book published.

I would like to thank Vincent Burke, for also proofreading my material.

I would like to thank my Sunday School class for listening to preclips of my book and encouraging me to complete the book.

Dedication

I dedicate this book to my late husband, Comadore Nicks, you were there for me. You inspired me with your wisdom and your calm but stern advice. Do not worry about what others think of you, just make sure that you think good of yourself. If you do what is right, you will always be pleased with yourself. Thank you, Baby.

I also dedicate this book to my birth mother, Mary Frances Yarbrough Elliott, whom I graced my first-born daughter, with this precious name. I did not have the chance to know you, therefore I was inspired to write this book to acknowledge to this audience how difficult life can be without your mother.

PROLOGUE

No matter what is written; just know this, that My God has bought me through many things in my life. It is because of him that I can testify and declare victory over every demon, offenses, disappointments and perils.

Offenses must come; but blessed is he, who is not offended in me

How is it, that we can become offended in God? No one ever wants to admit that I am offened in him; that would go against what we were taught. We as the created have no right to be angry or offended at God. Oh, but I was and at times, I still struggle with the lack of understanding.

I lost my mother at the age of three. I barely remember her, but I gravely miss her. I have been asked; how do you miss someone you barely knew? Because rarely can you find an earthly human being that can love you like your mother. My family was somewhat like David's family; he had children by many wives. I chose David because it has been recorded of the deception and discord between siblings with the help of their mothers. The only difference was all of our mothers weren't present; my older siblings' mother and my mother were deceased. Even though I was reared in a Christian atmosphere; things were far from being perfect or what I would consider a normal family.

My father was a deacon, played the drums and led devotion nearly every Sunday. My stepmother, whom I referred to as mother, played the organ, was the minister of music and a soloist. My grandmother was the pastor and founder of Believers In Christ Tabernacle, and she also was a soloist and sang in a group. I was surrounded by church goers, but sometimes we focus our attention on everything and everyone except what and who we should focus on.

My birth mother was the daughter of the Pastor of the church we attended. Like Joseph, the son of Jacob, was sold into slavery by his jealous brothers (Genesis 37:18-20), there was invalid hatred and jealousy for my brother(who is three years my junior) and me. Many people were jealous simply because of their perception of what they thought we had, but little did they know about the truth.

Life at home was treacherous; you never knew who or what was being said to start confusion. It is devastating to a child to hear a parent state that it is something about you they cannot take and to have your sibling tell you; you think you better than us. Now mind you we all lived in the same house, ate the same food and went to the same school and church; how was I supposed to think I was better than them, it made no sense. I did not understand then, but now that I am older; I can only speculate that the purchase of clothing, Christmas gifts and staying with my grandmother during the summer made my family feel that my brother and I were being treated specially. I recall one particular sibling who often visited other people in which she would receive purchased items. She was a pretty girl with beautiful hair; therefore, some of the sisters in the church gravitated to her. I would share clothes, shoes and lunch money with her. But it seemed she thought it necessary to keep me in odds with mother.

I had a younger sibling that took pleasure in breaking toys

(especially my brother's toys) that were purchased by my grandmother while we were away for the summer. He would brag about the destruction knowing there were little to no consequences. Generally, when my brother and I brought this to my parents' attention, we were labeled as troublemakers for *"complaining"*. Most of the time my brother and I stayed in our rooms while the others siblings were downstairs laughing and talking and having a good time. When we decided to join the rest of the family, it suddenly became to crowded and noisy; everyone was sent to their rooms. Of course, that did not last long, as my siblings would slowly resume in the family room. Often my brother and I were left out of family functions for we were told the event did not concern us. Maybe it dd not. Perhaps, they were trying on clothes that had been purchased, or one of my siblings' relatives were visiting/ picking them up, or for any reason. The result was that my brother and I were excluded.

Many times, on Sundays my brother and I were made to go sit in the car to prevent us from speaking to our grandmother while the others ran around until we were ready to go home. This prevented us from receiving our weekly allowance; therefore, causing us to go a week without lunch. Other times, we were told that our grandmother was too busy for us, not to bother her; yet the others could speak to her. Not knowing the circumstance; our grandmother would be perturbed with my brother and me. In my mind I did not understand why adults could not figure out what was going on. My grandmother had to know there was a reason we were not coming to see her; unfortunately, she never did until my brother and I covertly went to see her on our own. When we explained the situation to my grandmother, matters changed immediately. Imagine the many lunches my brother and I missed before she was made aware of our plight. Here we had no mother to protect, to comfort, to encourage nor present as our confidant. My father was a hard worker. He would come home from work, eat dinner quickly, then head out to start picking up churchgoers for service. Then of course, he had to take them home after service. That left little time for my father to have with his family. My grandmother: being the pastor, had her hands full as well. Which left a small window for the cuddleling of a grandmother. Though there are many other examples, these are a few illustrations as to *Why* I was offended in God.

I was quiet, very reserved; yet it appeared that I was invisible to my family. I would often ask God why He let me live. I could not understand why he had to take my mother at such a young age. She was only 26 when she passed. I blamed many people, my mother, grandmother, father and God. I was angry with my mom for leaving me; angry with my grandmother for not wanting to take her to the hospital, angry with my father for the same reason and of course with God for taking her. Now of course no one knew I was angry with them except God. Now, let me explain what I mean when I say I was angry with my grandmother for not taking my mother to the hospital. Going to the hospital was not as prevalent in that day as it is now. Many people either used old wise tale remedies, or just trusted in God for their healing. So it was not negligence, but a choice that all three adults (mother, father, and grandmother) made. I was too young to know what was happening, or to decide on the matter. Not that it would have made a difference.

. My eldest brother lost his mom at childbirth. Though he never knew his mother, there was a voidance in his life. Instead of dealing with the absence, he fulfilled his life by becoming a menace. He was always in trouble. I could not understand why he did the things he did, but I understand now, he could not articulate the abandoned feeling that he was experiencing. All he knew to do was act upon that feeling; which, most of the time was negative. Although, I was not a menace like my brother; yet I was and am a menace to myself. I resolved my hurt and offense by being withdrawn, little self-worth and lack of confidence. Being a recluse has wounded me more than anyone else could hurt me. In comparison, my brother being a menace, including all the things he did were dismissed, forgotten or turned into a comic; however, my peril is like a deep wound. Much like an injury, you care for it, cleanse it and it turns to a scab. One would think that the sore is healing until something happens to reopened that wound . Reoccurrences of mistreatment to me and now, the domino effect to my children are the things that rip the scab off the wound.

Even though I aspired to have that mother-daughter relationship, the attempt was null. It was as if I was trying to pull taffy. You see, to pull taffy, your hands had to have the right amount of butter or oil, the right consistency and strength in your arms to complete the task. I suppose I did not have the right plateau, to mound above the situation. There was an underlining tension between us that I never understood. My father was always gone, picking up, visiting or helping somebody besides working. I was a very sad child, who could not gain acceptance nowhere around me. At the age of sixteen I went to live with my grandmother; it was better, but she too was busy. She was always counseling someone seemingly no matter the time of day. We could not have a decent breakfast on Saturdays without someone knocking on the door with a problem. She was a very compassionate person, and she had a sentimental weakness for those less fortunate. Many times, she would bring people into the home for some reason or another that needed a place to stay. I shared my bed or gave my bed to individuals less fortunate than me. As an adolescent transitioning in these phases with no explanation or understanding, once more, I felt I was insignificant, set aside and dumped in this world to survive on my own.

I can remember a time when there was a piece of pie that was mine. I had planned to eat it when I got home from church. Anyone that knows me knows that I loved my sweets. This young girl that was staying at the house saw me with the pie and decided she wanted the pie. I was not hearing that. I thought about that pie during the service and my taste buds were set to enjoy the pie. Of course, the girl went into a tantrum which incited the decision of me giving up my pie to her. I was highly insulted and angry because the child ended up wasting a good portion of the pie. In the end she did not like the pie. **How was I supposed to feel about that? I cannot enjoy something that was mine**? Instead, I had to watch as that child turned her nose up at the pie that she had a tantrum to get, leaving a dissatisfaction for her and me. I cannot express what I wanted to do with the pie and her.

So, with that situation and many other situations that transpired, I felt I was insignificant. I found myself, repeating the question, why am I here? I went through life, smiling on the outside, but walking in emptiness. When my father passed away my pain was enormous; I felt he really did not get the chance to know me. I redirected my pain and took solace in rearing my children because I had someone to love me. I poured all my love and attention into my children.

This is ironic, because growing up I always said I did not want children. I was afraid that I would not know how to love them. I did not want them to go through or feel how I felt. But motherhood is amazing. I loved those children with every fiber in my being. I really think that I went overboard in protecting them and seeing to it that no one mistreated them ; including their father. However, that did not last long for my children grew up, became independent and constituted lives for themselves. Of course, my children love me and I them; however, at some point productive children wing from their parents.

You must love yourself.

Ergo, I had to learn how to love **me.**

Why?

What had I done?

Do you like me?

If you loved me, why have you allowed these things to happen?

How do you encounter such a task, when you are faced with low-self-esteem, while you struggle with trust and confidence. I had no doubt believing that things would work for others, but for me it just didn't seem to happen. But I thank God through the struggles, heartaches, sadness and pain he brought me through even though inwardly I was still offended. God already knew what I would go through in life. He did not promise a bed of roses and no troubles, but he did promise that he would bring me through them. I am guilty of whimpering and whining because I could not see my end. God already knew my strength and my weaknesses;

therefore, he prepared me for the battles ahead. We all are conquerors in life, because our troubles make us strong.

I wasted precious years dwelling in the past, letting the present slip away and not focusing on the future. But God in his love and compassion has mercy on me daily. The thing that is so beautiful with God is you don't know at the time why these things are happening, but I can remember a time I was just bawling asking God why and what had I done and why did he not like me. There was no justification in my mind how he could love me, while all these things were happening. After I finished bawling, I fell asleep and I dreamed I was on a beach, the water was beautiful, and it was so peaceful. I believe he was reminding me of the poem, about the footprints in the sand. Because when I looked down at the sand, I could see footprints in the sand. Like the poem, there were two sets of footprints, then one. I can remember thinking hum! Where did the other set go. I then heard a voice say" you are being carried, for the load is too heavy for you". I woke up rejoicing because I knew he was talking to me. He let me know that I have your daughter no matter what. My purpose for writing this book is to encourage others. No matter how dark life seems, our Father in Heaven and maker has given you the strength to make it through. "...God's strength is made perfect in weakness 2 Corinthians 12:9"

COME TAKE A JOURNEY WITH ME

This book is written based on a true story of my life as a child growing up in a family that had three sets of children: all with the same father, but different mothers. I will change the names of the characters as I see the need to mention a name simply for the privacy of the real characters that have not given me permission to use their names.

I simply want to tell my story and give details of highlighted episodes of my life. Unfortunately, in every story there are people that cross your path that may or may not enhance your life. Some encounters enhance your journey, to give you guidance or direction; other encounters are deterrence to hinder you, while yet, others are there to steady your steps while you try to figure out which direction you should take.

I should hope that this book will encourage those that have similar experiences. I trust that after reading this book, you will not allow your bad experiences to hinder you from becoming a total success. Do not allow your experiences to cripple your decisions, to excel to your potential which was ordained for you; nor do you succumb to life's ugliness, that will try to snatch your success, as a lion snatches its prey. I also hope it will help someone who has found themselves behaving in the manner as described in this book and maybe it could shine a light on your behavior and cause you to change how you treat others.

At any rate I pray that I can help someone mend their broken hearts, become aware of other feelings and forgive those who mistreat you. It is all in God's will that we may live in peace with ourselves and others.

CHAPTER ONE

LIFE AS A CHILD

Through the lens of a child life was sweet. I lived in the house with my parents, older siblings from my father's previous marriage, grandmother and cousins. The house was divided by several big sheets on a line where my cousins lived on one side and the rest of us lived on the opposite side. There was a big potbelly stove in the middle of a large room, assuming it to be the living room. I would take comfort in sitting on the floor watching the flames, as well as enjoying the heat. I could see the flames flashing, through the small openings in the design of the rod iron door of this stove. We would put big pans of water on the top of the stove to heat for bathing, washing dishes and clothes. I do not recall if that was a permanent thing or just temporary. I can remember vividly an incident that happened as I was sitting on the floor enjoying the heat from the stove that left an impression on me. There was a lot of sickness in the house. Some of my cousins were sick, as well as my oldest sister, who I will call (Bea). I do not recall if it was an epidemic or not, but what I do recall is my grandmother relentlessly putting big pans of water on that potbelly stove, putting some type of solvent in the water and boiling sheets, towels, pajamas and blankets when the beds were stripped. I can remember the fresh linen smell and the aroma of cleaning products that made the house feel clean and cozy.

During this period, some of Bea's relatives were upset with my grandmother, because she did not take her to the doctor.

My grandmother was a woman of faith who believed in the healing through Jesus Christ. The displeased relatives came to the house escorted by policemen to force my grandmother to take my sister to the hospital. I remember that the officers went all through the house on both sides. They returned to the living room, and said," Ma'am we do not see anything wrong. You have sanitized the entire house. We do not know how you are able to do this but continue to do as you are doing." Thank goodness in that era, the government did not interfere in parental guidance unless there was a noticeable appearance of neglect. The officers left. My grandmother then turned to Bea's relatives, pointed to the front door, and in a stern deep voice ordered them to get out and never to return.

Looking back on that situation, I could imagine how my sister's relatives felt; a family member of theirs (my sister's mother) had died during childbirth with her baby brother. They were left with unanswered questions and now, alienated from their nieces, nephews, and future great nieces and nephews. After all, the children were the only thing left of their deceased loved one.

Was there a better way to handle the dispute?
Was there even a dispute?
I was too young to know if there were previous discussions about taking my sister to the doctor. It would seem that, that should have been a discussion between my father and his in-laws. He was the father, which meant his decision should have been final. Perhaps, my father's decision seemed negligent to the in-laws and they decided to move forward with their plan. Their plan seemed to backfire. The problem with the in-laws, bringing the Police Officers to the house,

involved my grandmother. She should not have been involved; however, we all lived with her. The perception was that you brought the police against my grandmother, and not my father, because he was at work. He was unaware of the debacle going on at the house. You see, the only reason my father was at this residence was because he had married my mother. It was not uncommon for many families to live together. The economy was not great and even less for those of color. So our family, which was a blended family, consisted of his children(children from a previous marriage) and their children,(my father, mother, my two siblings and me), and my cousins , which consisted of a father, mother and four children. We all lived with my maternal grandmother.

During the 1930's and maybe further back than that, there was a separation between family members that had been spiritually born and those who were called " *the unsaved*". The Pentecostal Apostalic way of life incurred a strict doctrine that had ritualistic structures that drew a contour line between the "saved" and "unsaved". My sister's relatives were considered the "unsaved". Therefore, communications were lost with many family members. I could see how easily one would think that their kin were in a cult and felt desperate to get them out. I really believe this was a desperate attempt which made the situation worse. Not only did they lose contact with their family, my father had soon remarried and moved on with his life; leaving a void and again unanswered questions, to them that were connected through his late wife. I am not aware of the time that past before my older siblings reconnected with the family members. I can only pray that there was a rekindling with their family. I am reminded and have recorded this example, as I had never experienced such magnitude of anger from my grandmother.

This was significant to me, because I would sit and watch my grandmother, she always seemed sweet and kind. To describe my grandmother I would say there was peace and tranquility surrounding her. She had this beautiful smile and spoke in authority, but with assurance that all was well.

The household seemed peaceful and full of laughter. There was the sound of children playing and enjoying themselves; conversations of the adults ending in whistles of joy. I was told that I could get a little feisty when I was spanked. They say I would run to my mom like I was going to hit her; consequently I am sure that I learned a valuable and long-lasting lesson that hitting parents is prohibited in a structured family. Of course, I do not remember that, as I was too young. I do not ever remember hearing shouting and arguments. It was just an aroma of love, peace and joy. Along with the sensational smell of food and desserts cooking. It was just, as I can recall, being only three a wonderful life. Which reminds me, I was told, that I loved Christmas lights. They said we would go riding, just to view the decorations displayed on our neighbor's homes. As we would ride, I was told, I would holler out wonderful, beautiful repeatedly. Of course, it was in a three-year old's pronunciation as, "wonderful, beautiful. I guess I have not relinquished that love for Christmas. It is my favorite time of year.

The sound in the air was filled with music of old spiritual hymns, Mahalia Jackson, James Cleveland and many others. I vaguely remember a young child who loved to sing, stomp his feet and clap his hands. He was a jolly little fellow with big pretty dimples when he smiled. Sam, I will call him, was between my younger brother, Greg, and me. I do not remember if the time frame of my sister being sick, was the same time that little Sam was sick. All I know is Sam passed.

I suppose he could have passed, around the same time my mom passed or a little before. There was a pandemic, called Tuberculosis. I was told this was the cause of my mom's passing. Though I am not certain, I do know Sam was not around very long. My baby brother, Greg, was only four months when my mom passed. Therefore, Sam could not have been more than fourteen to eighteen months old when he passed, because I was three. I do not recall the time frame, but I recall seeing a small oblong object draped with cream lining that looked soft like crepon. It was sitting on a table; whether that table was in the home or at a funeral home I do not recall; however, I believe it was in the home. Viewings at the resident's home was common. I, also, recall being picked up so that I could view a body in a casket which had to be my mother. The memory of my mother is obscure. One thing that has always puzzled me was why I could not remember much about my mother, yet, I could very vividly remember another lady that I was around. Later as an adult, I described the features of this lady to my grandmother and summoned to understand this lady's connection. Her explanation was that I frequently stayed with this lady. As to why I stayed with this lady, that was never explained. I could speculate but I will not for it seemed this lady was a mystery. I cannot speak any derogatory remarks against this evidently care giver, because I can only remember how sweet and kind she was to me.

Chapter Two

The Sudden change in my life

Like a blink of an eye, I was in a totally different environment. That warm sweet cozy feeling was gone, as though I was snatched out of a story book into a different life. A life that was not pleasant, rather dark and gloomy. I was a bruised child, that had lost her mother at the tender age of three; thrust into a family that was as deceitful as a mirage in the desert in the noonday sun. Struggling with the memories of a wonderful life that was swopped away like a wind storm that left nothing but fragments of unbelief. Everything that **used to be** was gone forever as if it had never been. My mother,(whom I will call Margret) barely mentioned, and even at times forbidden to be mentioned as if she was a plague.

Was there a secret?

What were they hiding?

What was the mystery?

I was told that my mother had Tuberculosis. This was a pandemic disease in that era. I don't know if at the time, that my mother was sick with this disease, if there was a mandatory quarantine or not. I do know that in later years, anyone stricken with this disease, had to be quarantined. This was a very contagious disease. However, I know my mother did not go to the hospital, so perhaps the whole house was under quarantine during this time. Maybe this was the same time that my sister (Bea) was sick. It would make sense that Bea's relatives would come with police escort if they believed my mother had Tuberculosis and the house was under quarantine.

The home was unfriendly and cold. Whispers, that were chilling, yet, subtle as an owl, watching in the midnight shadow of the moon. Where did it all go and why did it have to end? As a child I was devastated. By now , I was about four and can remember more of life's episodes. I can remember my brother Greg, seemingly living the majority of his time in his baby bed. Greg was so unhappy. I felt so sad for him because he cried a lot. I became his little mother. I would remove him from his bed, clean his little face , change his diaper and dress him. I remember sitting upstairs in my room alone while others were downstairs laughing and talking. When I decided to join them suddenly it became crowded and too noisy. We were all ordered to go to our rooms. Unfortunately, my brother, Greg, and I were the only ones who made it back to our rooms. I would visit Greg's room, or he would come to mine. We would talk about how sad we were. We wished that we could live again with our grandmother. Sometimes when I came home from school, I would just go in my room lay on my bed and cry. It was not because I was sick, or hurt, just because I was sad. It felt like I did not belong there. By this time my father was remarried and had started a family with his third wife. It seemed that I was farther in the shadow of no ones mind. I only existed because I was given birth by my parents. There were times I thought, "if only I could have passed with my mother and brother Sam". But then I would think of Greg. "Oh no, I could not leave him alone". We have been the backbone of our survival. We were always together; therefore, together we would get into trouble. It did not seem so bad as long as the two of us were together. Together we adapted to the situation and made life durable sufficiently to overcome many obstacles.

Now, understand, life was not all doom and gloom, for there were times of laughter and playfulness, because children will adapt to their environment. Sitting around the table with just one glance at a sibling would cause laughter even when you did not know what you were laughing about. What was worse, was trying to hold your laugh, when you were suddenly given that unapproved glance from your father. My brother, who I will call (Phil) was hilarious. He could make you laugh and then look away, making you look like something was wrong with you. Especially, in the presence of our father. I can recall a few times that happened and dad would say, **"Marcia, are you ready for the rubber room"?** Meaning , **are you going crazy?** All you could say was **,"no sir".** Then the other siblings, would go off to a corner where dad could not see them and laugh. Many mornings especially on Saturday and Sundays I was the last to leave the table because we were having oatmeal for breakfast and I despised oatmeal. I would hold one spoon in my mouth for ever trying to swallow the oatmeal. Finally, Greg, would rescue me by sneaking back and eating my breakfast. Sometimes I would run to the bathroom and spit the oatmeal in the toilet without getting caught. What ever was served for breakfast or dinner was what you ate. There were no different foods prepared. If you did not like the food or did not want what was prepared, you missed your meal.

Just as much as I hated oatmeal; I loved milk, but of course it was rationed because there were many mouths to feed. There were times I would sneak into the kitchen and get some milk. One time I was almost caught so, I threw the milk behind the washing machine. A few days later I remembered how spoiled milk smelled. I knew I had to clean that milk up. I decided to go back and clean up the milk. I climbed on top of the washing machine to reach the spilled milk; unfortunately, the washing machine had a glass top. Immediately, my knee went through the glass, shattering the top to the washing machine and causing a big gash in my knee. Naturally I was scolded because I had broken the glass on the machine, but I do not recall any attention to the bleeding knee other than, "that is good enough for you; you had no reason for being there". Little did they know I had a reason, but refused to explain that reason. I did not want the smell of spoiled milk to permeate the laundry room and kitchen. Eventually I was able to drink more milk because, the government issued vouchers for large families to receive powdered milk, eggs, cheese and butter. The cheese and butter was good , but the milk and eggs took some doing to acquire the taste. Eventually I learned to make the milk satisfactory to eat with cereal and drink with plenty of strawberry flavored powder. I loved fixing grilled cheese sandwiches with the cheese , and loads of butter on the toasted bread. We would also get the big bags of rice, flour , cornmeal and sugar. Those items you had to put in brown gunny sacks to keep those little beetle bugs out.

Over all we made the best of what we had. My sister and I ,(who I will call Charity), would get into the kitchen and cook dinner for everyone. We would team up and make desserts to sell. We had plenty of orders from church, school and Bea's job. I can remember especially around Thanksgiving and Christmas. We had orders for rolls, different types of cookies,(especially the Mexican wedding cake cookies), cakes(coconut, lemon and german chocolate) and pies, (coconut cream and lemon meringue). The kitchen was filled with the aroma of baked goods. I do not recall what we did with the money made from the bake sales. What ever was purchased we both enjoyed; simply because we purchased the items with our money. Charity and I baked together for several years, until Charity started working and eventually moved into her own place. Things never stay the same, because time moves everyone forward, willingly or not.

Now lets move on to discuss one of the worst under developed and under sights that a contractor or designer could ever neglect when designing home structures. When I was growing up most of the homes that I lived in and visited no matter how elegant, had one (1) bathroom. To find a home with two bathrooms; you lived in luxury. So therefore, the bathroom was a huge issue. Can you imagine a household of seven or eight with one bathroom? There was always a line waiting to utilize the bathroom. The model of homes in that day was not conducive to large families. Why on earth would anyone design a home with one bathroom and that being next to the kitchen? More times than none, the smell of the refuse waste, coming from the bathroom overpowered the aroma of food cooking in the kitchen. It seemed obvious, that every time the kitchen was occupied to prepare food; so was the bathroom.

" Oh my word, would you flush the toilet and spray please?"

That was the familiar cry from the cook in the kitchen. Why did it seem that the men folks would smell the worst and would exclaim, **"I don't want the water to splash on me"**?

The next **SHOUT** was, **"Boy you better flush that toilet ; NOW!!!"**.

That was a constant battle.

Have you ever been out somewhere and suddenly felt a strong urge to have a bowel movement. No bathroom in sight and the muscles in your rectum seem to be loosing grip? You think any moment now, you are going to experience incontinence by making a mess on yourself and anything nearby. As you are pressing with all your strength, tears running down your face and moving as fast as you can towards a restroom; then, with a stroke of luck you are able to relieve yourself. That was the horrible experience time and time again living in a house with one bathroom. I remember times I would be on the floor begging " God please let them come out please". Again, I do not know why it was the male species that occupied the bathroom the longest. What on earth were they doing?

At some point in this particular house the bathroom door got a little peep hole. I do not know when, nor how a hole became in the bathroom door; I just remember seeing my siblings looking in a hole while someone was in the bathroom. I too, found myself looking in the hole at my siblings and a gentleman that stayed with us for a few months, but never my parents.   At that time, it was nine of us that had to share one bathroom and now this man made ten. Somehow, I felt justified looking in on him because he was invading our space. The siblings that we spied on, was a form of getting even, because they would spy on you. I recall times I was dancing around in the bathroom trying to pull my pants down and placing my finger over the hole all at the same time. That was a sight and almost a mishap. I do not know if that hole was ever fixed, because not long after that, I went to live with my grandmother. Now, as far as the person living in our home; this seemed to be a periodic thing. At some point in my twelve years living with my father and stepmother we had our paternal grandmother(Martha), aunt and two children, an uncle and now this gentleman living with us. None of them stayed for a long period of time, except our grandmother.

We had a shed in the backyard that was no longer being used. My father and brothers turned that shed into a living quarter for our grandmother. There was space for a small refrigerator to keep drinks and food . She had her own bathroom and of course a bedroom/living room. We would take her food, if she did not feel up to coming into the house. Grandmother Martha, was part Indian. She had beautiful smooth skin with the high cheek bone and long cold black hair. She would often ask me to wash and comb her hair. I loved doing that task, because I felt that connection as grandmother and granddaughter. Feeling a connection was something I seldom felt. In the summer, she loved sitting on the front porch. We lived across the street from a park. The swimming pool was right in front of our house. So, grandmother Martha, enjoyed watching the children play in the swimming pool. I remember one day as she was sitting on the porch, Greg and I came out to sit on the porch as well. Greg, of course did not sit for long. He was up jumping around and playing. Our neighbor two doors down started playing music, which could be heard, probably throughout the neighborhood. Greg started moving with the music doing some kind of dance. Grandmother Martha started clapping her hands, stomping her feet and shouting with her high pitch, but small volume voice, demanding Greg to stop what he was doing. Greg, stopped what he was doing, but the two of us was almost running each other over, trying to get out of the sight of grandma, so we could laugh. The picture of all the commotion was overwhelming, and we could not hold our laugh. I am laughing still today as I write and replay that episode in my mind.

As I previously stated, there were good memories at this house, as well. On occasions when my father had a good month of pay, he would stop by Dairy Queen and bring us each a Dilly Bar. Oh, how we loved Dilly Bars and looked forward to receiving them. Somehow the word would get out that he was going to bring them when he came home. We would all be standing in the kitchen waiting patiently for him. This was a treat, because this did not happen often. It was about seven or eight of us children. I do not remember how much Dilly Bars cost, but he had to buy quite a few. Sometimes he would play with us. Pretending that he did not have anything. He would look at us, and ask "why are you all standing in the kitchen like ducklings?"

We would laugh and respond, "did you bring the Dilly Bars?"

My father, the prankster, would have either left them in the vehicle or on the night stand in the living room, then he would say "I don't have any Dilly Bars what are you talking about?" Our little faces would droop.

All of a sudden, my father would appear with the Dilly Bars and laughing all the while. My father could be loads of fun at times and others times seemed so occupied that you felt invisible in his presence. This was a common characteristic of a responsible man in a large structured family trying to make ends meet. Most of the time he was either at work or out helping others. My father drove the church bus, visited the sick or he was found lending a hand to someone, somewhere.

As long as I can remember he was a Deacon in the church and soon became Head Deacon. These positions came with responsibilities and time away from the family. In hindsight,

I know he was doing what he believed was right . Children do not understand the terms "working for the Lord "or " doing what is right". As a child, I longed for more of his presence. He really tried to keep all of his children together, to rear us in the fear and admonition of God, as he took us to church to hear the word of God. I can only imagine what he went through losing two wives in a span of five years with five children left to rear. Two of those children were infants when their moms passed and none of us over twelve years of age. That was a challenge, yet he continued to work and be present in church activities. With the passing of his two wives, he married rather quickly. Leaving no time to morn or adjust. I have often wondered , if marring each wife so soon after his previous wife had passed was more convenience or a way of life in the church. I do know there were challenges, hardships and heartaches.

CHAPTER THREE

MY SCHOOL DAYS

When I started school we lived in a house that was a duplex. There was a living quarter upstairs and one downstairs. Our family lived in the unit upstairs and my cousins lived in the downstairs unit. I started kindergarten at the age of four in September of 1955. I can remember some of the outfits I wore. I had these corduroy jumpers that had a pocket on the bib almost as big as the bib itself with blouses that had little characters on one and fruits on the other. I had other dresses, skirts and tops, but I loved those outfits I do not know why but I did. I remember walking to school with my older siblings, after they returned home for lunch. I could hardly wait until they got home for lunch because, I knew I would be going with them when they returned to school for the afternoon. I looked to my older sister, Bea, for support. I felt safe with her. That did not last long because she soon went to a different school because of our age difference. The good thing about that, was that we still walked in the same direction for school, she just had to walk further going to high school. I remember one day, as I was walking home from school; there was a commotion going on ahead of where I was. I enquired about the commotion and was told that it was a fight. As I approached I realized it was Bea, in the fight. This girl that was fighting Bea, was much bigger and taller. The girl was dragging Bea and pulling handfuls of hair out of Bea's head. I knew I was much younger than Bea, but could not stand to see what was happening. I ran and jumped up on the girl's back and sunk my teeth in her back. The more the girl squirmed and hollered, the harder I bit. When she finally shook me off, she took off running. And never bothered any of us again.

As I mentioned, the house was a duplex with living quarters upstairs and down. We lived upstairs with a front and back stair case. The back stairs was long and dark. In the spring and fall there were caterpillars that crawled up and down those stairs. I was scared to death of those nasty things. My worst fear was that one would fall on me and as life would have it, one did. I thought I was going to lose my mind. I start removing my clothes right there out side and the scream was chilling. After that, I had to be threatened, to receive a spanking, to go down those stairs. Mind you, that was the entrance and exit we were allowed to come into or depart from the house. We were forbidden to use the front entrance. Why, I have no clue. It was just a rule. I cried bloody murder every time I had to go down those stairs. It did not help, that I had a brother that always teased me, as though he was going to throw one on me. He never did, because he knew I would go berserk on him. After getting pass the stairs ordeal, my day was good. Boy, was I glad when we moved away from that place.

I enjoyed going to school , but was bothered about the fact of, leaving Greg home. He seemed all alone. He would be in his baby bed just crying. I would always go to him and say" don't cry brother, I love you". He always had a sad look on his face. When I started to go to school for the full day I was really sad for Greg, because he would be in the babybed crying when we left in the morning and when we returned in the evening he would still be in the babybed. He was always glad when we got home. This went on, until he finally, learned how to climb out of the babybed. I do not know what happened when we were in school other than his account of events. They were not pretty. I will not go into that because that would be his story. I became his little mother and protector, always fixing his pants and making sure his face was clean and noise wiped. I would fight like a mother protecting her cubs, if anyone made trouble with him. The two of us were a pair. Greg was, tickled pink, as the old folks would say, when he was old enough to go to school and by then the younger siblings were old enough to be his playmate. He loved to eat. His face would light up when the food was done and the announcement was made that it was time to eat. He was a growing boy and food just seem to escape to his feet. In other words he was always ready to eat. Because of his love to eat he was called a pig by Charity. She also loved to keep trouble going with mother and me. Charity would lie, saying I had said this or that when I had not. She would do things and blamed me, no matter how many times I denied doing them, she was always right. Therefore I would be punished instead of her. I can remember one time ,that she did not get away with blaming me. Charity and I shared a bed; though neither of us were bed wetters; this particular time she wet the bed. She tried her best to blame me, stating, I wet on her, but fortunate for me she was the one wet and I was not. So that did not go well with her that time. So, she was the one who had to strip the bed and wash everything.

My grandmother purchased Greg and my clothes, for birthdays, school and Christmas. She also purchased toys at Christmas. I do not know if this was an arrangement with my father and my grandmother; trying to help him with responsibilities. I do know, his responsibilities were great;

clothing and caring for the five of his children, and now other children were being born with his present wife. This caused a dissension for Greg and I with the others. When you are a child you do not think about consequences and feelings that others may have in certain situations. We just looked forward to the new clothes and other amenities that we received. Although I shared my clothes with Charity; she was small and petite, so she could wear some of my clothes, that was not satisfying. She still did not seem to care for me. When my siblings would get new clothes for school; they would all be in the family room receiving their clothes, Greg and I had to stay in our rooms, we could not be part of that moment. Now by this time the younger siblings were receiving clothing and gifts from relatives of their mother and Charity was always receiving gifts from church members. As a child I felt as if I had done something wrong and was being punished, but in hindsight maybe no harm was meant because most of the time Greg and I would receive new clothes while visiting our grandmother.

Many times while visiting our grandmother during holiday and summer breaks, items that Greg and I previously received were destroyed. We would receive a scolding when we inquired on the matter. We were told not to return causing problems because there was peace while we were gone. As if we were the source of the problem. What made it worse, was, we were teased about what was destroyed, and there was no possible solution, other than taking the lost. We even tried to hide items to no avail. Sometimes we would go to our oldest sister to complain about the situation, but it was not much she could do. She would just try to console us and say you will just have to let it go. Well there were times I just did not want to let it go. I would grab that sibling before

I knew what I was doing and either hit, scratch or choked him. Then I would have to brib him with candy to stop him from reporting what I had done. Greg would laugh at me, he would say "you let your temper get the best of you". And yes! I guess I had. Now my older sister Bea, I loved her. She took time to talk to me, give me advice, and she would give me chores to do for her, and she would pay me. She was the one that explained to me what it was and what to do when I came into womanhood. Bea never got angry with me when I would sneak and wear some of her clothes. She had this half slip that was called a crinoline petticoat. I was always sneaking that to wear to school. I loved how it made my dress or skirt stand out. She would just tell me to wash it and put it back. Eventually she moved into her own place.

Now this left Charity and I, being the older girls in the house, to bond together after a few years. We would walk to school together. We still had to walk to school, even though we were in a different house. The school we attended was in the opposite direction of the previous school we attended. Sometimes we would come across bullies, that would not take leave me alone, for an answer. My father was one who did not like for us to fight. As a matter of fact it was forbidden. Sometimes no matter how you tried to avoid confrontation; you had those who would not leave you alone. One day Charity came home from school and she was upset. I enquired about why she was upset. She explained there was this girl in her class that picked with her. I asked her why? She said, " because I will not say anything back to her when she accosted me. I do not want to get in trouble." A few days later as Charity and I were walking home from school, Charity heard someone call her name. When she turned to see who called her, it was the girl she spoke of. Charity said, "Marcia, that is the girl I told you about." Charity said, "I am tired of her messing with me. I will throw her down." Charity did not have to say another word. We waited until the girl came up to put her hands on Charity; Charity grab her , threw her down and I pounced on her. I grabbed her head and held it in the snow. The more she moved the more I pushed; until I heard someone say," stop, you going to smother her." I guess Charity did not realize the strength I had. From that day forward we did not have anyone bothering us. When my father heard about it, he was angry, but I did not receive the corporal punishment, just a good scolding. Charity did speak up and said , " but dad the girl kept picking with me and she was getting ready to do it again, when she called my name. Dad finally said with coherse from mother and the children's echo, " well alright, but I do not want to here of anyone of you starting a fight." YES! That is all I needed. I never bothered or started anything with anyone.

I was in seventh or eighth grade. My home room was in a home economics room. It had a small fitting room in the corner of the room. Because it was a home room, male and female we in the room. Many time the home room teacher came in late; which left space for a lot of folly to go on. When I speak of folly, the boys would take a girl in the fitting room and would have sex with them. This particular boy decided that it was my turn. Now, we girls being silly would go in that room to comb our hair getting ready for the next round of classes, because it had mirrors in there. This particular day, I decided to go in with other girls to recomb my hair. Suddenly , this boy appeared in the room. The other girls ran out, held the folding door so I could not get out. Well, I was faced with a dilemma. Either I give in, to this creep or I fight my way out. Well I chose the latter. I warned him not to come any closer to me. Well, because I was quiet and did not bother anyone, I guess the boy thought he had me. What he did not know, that I was like a tiger, if you cornered me. I waited until he got in arms length. I through a punch at him with all my might. Knocked him to his knees. We burst that door down fighting like two males. Mind you, I never had a problem with males or females from that day forward. Of course, I was labeled as the crazy girl. But it was ok, because everyone had heard of what had happened and would not bother any of us again.

Now to get back to the fight I had with my male classmate. When the teacher finally decided to come in the room , the fight was well in force. After he broke up the fight , he order us to write on the board. ***I will not fight.*** I refused to do the exercise. I was not going to be punished for protecting myself. When I got home I called my maternal grandmother and explained the situation to her. She then called my dad and explained to him what had happened. I did not get into trouble for that episode. Although dad was not to keen on me disobeying the teacher, but he understood. Now for a whole year , after the episode with the classmate and I fighting; things went well at school. I was the one the principle or other teachers would call to give a report to our parents, because the two brother, Phil and Greg were acting up in school. Of course, I would not say anything unless they sent a note home to be signed. Just about two months before graduation from the eighth grade another episode happened. There was a new Health teacher that took the place of the old Health teacher that had retired six months prior. This teacher was young, fresh out of college, and inexperience in dealing with students. For the last three weeks of school our class had rotated to Health . Now, in previous health classes, when the class read lessons from a book, near the end of the class the teacher would select a student to collect the books. Being students with a lot of folly, if someone was still reading in the book; the student who was collecting the book would gently snatch the book. They would both laugh and move on to the next student. This particular day we were reading books. I did not hear the teacher tell us to close our books. On top of that, I had not gotten glasses which I desperately needed. The next thing I knew, the book was being snatched. I honestly thought it was a classmate, so I held the book. When I let the book down and realized it was the teacher; I was getting ready to say I was sorry, I thought she was a classmate. When suddenly she yanked the book from me, closed it and slapped me with the book in my face. If you have heard the phrase, "I saw stars." Well let me tell you, I literally saw stars. Black and white objects were dancing around in my head.

The event that I am about to tell, is from the account of witnesses. I can not give you my account because I do not know. I blacked out. I was told that I snatched that teacher and worked her over pretty good. Now I recall sitting directly in the middle of a u shape desk arrangement. I do not know if I pulled the teacher over the desk, if I myself jumped over the desk or I pushed the desk up or back. Either way we made contact away from the desk. The next thing I remember we were in the hall. I could hear someone calling me, but it sounded as if they were far away. When I came to myself, I looked down and the teacher was on the floor. It took me a minute to grasp what was, or had happened. I naturally had to go to the principal's office, who called home and talked to mother. I was still in a daze, but heard the principal say that this was grounds for me to be sent to juvenile center.

Evidently, mother must have ask the principle, what was I doing. I heard the principle say that I was standing there in a daze like I had no care in the world. I was sent home. While walking home I noticed that my face was aching, and the thought ran across my mind, boy are you in trouble; yet I was not too concern. I was still trying to figure out what happened. When I approached the door, mother was standing there to open the door. When she opened the door, she let out a holler. It scared me so bad, because I did not know what to think. Immediately she called my maternal grandmother and they both called the principal. They wanted to know who was this teacher. What I did not know was that my face was so swollen on that one side that it was causing me to look deformed. When it was all said and done , the teacher was reprimanded and put on probation, I of course, could not go back to the class . That was ok because I only had three weeks before graduation. This episode did not effect me graduating. Thank goodness.

On Sundays Greg and I would receive an allowance for the week from my grandmother. I can remember to this day the amount. We would receive five dollars a week. Many times we would be sent to the car while the others were still playing around the church until my father and step mother were ready to go home. This prevented Greg and I from speaking to our grandmother and of course not receiving our allowance. This was not too bad as long as we were going to grade school because we would walk home from school for lunch. When I started going to high school this was a problem because this meant I had no money for lunch. Many weeks I went without lunch because of no allowance. On the other hand, my grandmother did not know that we were being kept from seeing her and she thought Greg and I were ignoring her. So therefore the allowance was not sent to us. I asked my dad one time for some money for lunch and I got a lecture on how hard it was," to come by money" as he would put it. So that was not an option. Maybe he did not have it or maybe he knew if he gave one he would have to give to others and that would be too much for him. Either way, I was out of luck if I did not get that allowance. I guest one would try to figure out how could five dollars be enough for lunch for a week. I would actually spend less than a dollar a day. I could get a meal, a drink and maybe a dessert, according to what was being served. Some times I would eat a light lunch, so that I could save money for something else I wanted, like candy ,chips or a soda from the super market. It did not take a lot of money because I could get a nice bag of candy for twenty five cents and chips and sodas were a nickel. It was not until sometime later that Greg and I was able to explain to our grandmother that we were not ignoring her only being prevented from seeing her.

Not long after that I bribed my grandmother in coming to live with her. Not really, but I did tell her, while I was there for the summer, that I could not go back home. Of course she questioned me for my reason. Though I felt I could not indulge into the depth of what was going on, I was serious enough for her to take note. Through my tears, I told her if she made me go back I would run away. Now, she was not going to allow me to run away and mind you, I had no idea where I would go. But I felt I could no longer endure staying there. Was I beaten or starved? No, not at all. It was the cunning ways and underhanded things that were done. There were comments made, that caused me to feel uncomfortable as if I was not wanted. I felt I was in the way. I longed for a women that I barely knew, yet I missed her dearly. I would lay awake at night and cry. I remember at times asking, " why did you leave Greg and me, did you not love us enough to go to the hospital and be healed"? I would tell her how I felt unloved and unwanted. I even asked her why did she birth me into the world only to leave me. If a child has no protection of a mother, it feels valnerable to physical or emotional harm. No where to go for solace or comfort. You stand as prey to any vulture ready to attack whether physical or mental. Sometimes I wonder if that was the reason I married so young.

I went to live with my grand mother the summer after my sixteen birthday. My sixteenth birthday was the first time I had a birthday party. It was not like birthday parties like today, where you invite your friend and close relatives. This was just with my siblings and a few people that lived in my grandmother's house. The party was at my grandmother's. While we were conversating and eating , a question came up pertaining to a couple that was dating. This was odd, because children where not included in adult conversations. Although I was sixteen and had a couple of siblings older than me, we were still consider as children, in that day in time. We were asked our opinion about this particular couple. Well, my sister, Charity and I voiced our opinion. Not to leave you in the dark, of what the question pertained to, we were asked if we thought this couple should be together. My sister and I said, no along with other comments. Oh boy, that infuriated my father. When we returned home, he called the whole family together, and he scolded us. As we were all standing there listening to my father, of course doing everything we could to keep from laughing, because he was so upset. All it would take was for one of us to make eye contact with another and it would have been chaos. The laughter would began. But during his lecture, my father got so caught up that he referred the couple as one, a puppy and the other a horse. Now let me clarify, He was not calling them this. What he was trying to expound to his children, that no matter what a person look like or what one does, it was not our place to make a comment even though we were asked. Of course, the lecture was over, because everyone burst into laughter to the point that even my father had to laugh. He said, "you all are so silly , get out of here", **here,** meaning his room.

At the end of the summer vacation, after I turned sixteen, I permanently lived with my grandmother. My dad was sad and probably a little hurt, but my stepmother seemed more angry. She accused me of wanting to go live with my grandmother so I could have access to my boyfriend. She also told me that I was going to get pregnant. She did not know , that very statement , made me determine, that I would not fall prey to her negative statement made against me . I was a little confused, as to her concern, since she was the one who made the statement , that it was something about me she could not take. I thought she would be please that she no longer had to take me, what ever that meant. I know I was certainly happy that I would no longer have to endure ,Mamma Bee, as I called her, just tolerating me. I would be in an environment that was calm and serene. Although I had to care for myself, as far as being responsible for getting to school, doing home work and keeping my clothes clean by washing them on hand ,because there was not a washing machine or dyer; I did not mind because the atmosphere was great.

I remember a particular morning in the winter, I got up for school. I mentioned the winter because it was still dark in the mornings. I guess I was exhausted because I looked at the clock wrong. I would normally get up around 6:15 to get ready and be at the bus stop by 7:00. The bus would come at 7:10. Well this morning I got up an hour earlier. I noticed that the sky was slightly darker than usual. Normally at 7:00 the day was beginning to dawn. I still did not think anything was wrong. It wasn't until the bus never arrived that I suspected something was wrong. So, I went back home, only to find that it was only 6:30. Then, I got scared, because I realized that it was quite early for me to be out by myself. Normally there would be others I could here coming behind me, to the bus stop. That alone should have alerted me that something was wrong. But as I said I must have been exhausted. In the Apostolic Church we had service Sunday morning and Sunday night. Sometimes service did not end until 10:30-11:00 a clock. Then I would have to complete some assignments . So getting into bed was late. Oh , another thing , I have never used an alarm clock to awaken me. I have always awaken on my own. There has only been a few times that I have experienced over sleeping. I could count them on one hand, but this particular time I awaken too soon. When I got home from school that day, my grandmother asked me," what was going on this morning?" I laughed and explained to her what I did. She laughed and told me to be careful. She also said she begin to pray for my safety. So , you see, it was all good because she prayed for my protection. And I **was** protected.

Chapter Four

My First Job While In School

Now that I was sixteen and living with my grandmother, life seemed fresh. It was quiet except for intermittent burst of laughter because something hilarious was said or demonstrated. I had paced myself to give more attention to my studies as well as sewing and going to church regularly. I was in my Junior year and all classes seemed to be intense. There were times I not only studied, but I prayed to pass certain classes. I Thank the Lord I passed. These are times that you begin to seek guidance from the Almighty. Parents or Guardians can only go so far to help. By the help of The Lord I was able to manage my grades. I decided to seek for employment. I discussed it with my grandmother and she gave me her approval.

It did not take long to find employment. I was hired at a store/restaurant in downtown Indianapolis named Kresges. I worked in the cafe' area. I worked with another sixteen year old who I knew from church. Incidentally this young man is who I end up marrying. We worked well together serving customers, listening to their small talk as we fixed their lunch and giving them feed back. Mostly, we were glad to make the customers happy so we could receive a nice tip. The customers enjoyed us working there, because we were giving them probably a double portion of what they were used to getting. They would order coneys and we would give them a nice amount of the meat sauce. The milk shakes, I am sure we gave them twice the amount of ice cream that had been allotted. But the customers loved us. We were told that they had an increase of customers in the Cafe' since the two of us were working there. We even receive a $.25 cent raise. I felt so proud when I received my first pay check. My check was around $155.

I worked for about 6 months . I enjoyed making my own money and feeling useful. I would get out of school , hurry to the bus stop, because I only had ten minutes until the bus came, and then head downtown to work. There were times when customers would be waiting for me or the young man to serve them. We had a lot of fun especially on the days that we were not busy. We would race to see who would get their chores done first. The last would have to buy the other a shake or drink. Of course the guy would always order the shake. Me I would go light and order a drink. I knew his money was much needed, mine was going in the bank or to purchase an item for someone. I was blessed enough that I did not need the money per-se. But on those busy days, we would work until the last customer left. Then we would have to clean up and close the registers . All of this we had to do within a certain time in order to catch that bus. If we missed the bus that meant another 30-45 minute wait. Which would get us home later and we would have less time to do homework. But we were young and vibrant so we did not fuss to much about the late days.

During the Christmas season we loved it. Yes we were tired, but we were happy because customers were more generous. They would leave big tips and sometimes would pay for our meals. It seemed like the time would go so fast. I suppose that was because we kept busy. During that time we would have our regular customers plus customers who had been shopping. They would be so hungry from shopping that they would have big orders. Usually, they would maybe order a drink and chips, or a shake . Occasionally, a customer would order a meal. But Christmas was different.

Just as things were getting good, one day during her Christmas shopping , my grandmother stop into Kresges. I was so busy , that I did not notice my grandmother standing a ways off watching me. She and her secretary finally approached the counter and order something to eat. I was surprised, but delighted to serve her. I thought she would be pleased with me, being a good worker, by caring for my customers. She ate her food while the secretary and she talked. The young man that worked their was also glad to see her. We spoke and conversate a little , but we were quite busy. Of course she left a big tip and waved goodbye. The young man and I had a good night. We both made a good amount of tips and we were happy. When I got home, tired and exhausted, ready to tackle homework so I could go to bed, my grandmother called me. When I went into her room she was kind of sad. I asked her if everything was alright? Her response was, " no baby, mama felt so bad for you working that hard. You do not have to work like a slave. You do not need money that bad. I want you to quit that job. I have some sewing that I need you to do for me. You can make more money sewing. You would not have to work that hard." I was so disappointed, but I knew I had to be obedient. After getting over the hurt and sulking, I learned that she was right. I did make more money sewing and it was not as stressful, but at the time I was enjoying what I was doing.

I just want to say , you may not always understand when circumstances come, because you think things are going well, but remember it pays off to be obedient to those who have rule over you. Being obedient saved me from being hurt. In the winter , as you know it gets dark early. When I was working I would get off the bus and it would be dark. I had to walk three blocks to get home. Thank God I was spared from being snatched and raped. For God watched over me. Maybe a year later after I had stopped working; there was an incident where a young lady that had come to our church was found dead. It was sad and scary because it was on a Sunday night that she was there. She came down to the alter for prayer. My grandmother , who was the pastor , took special note in her. My grandmother began to talk with the young lady. She expressed the need for the young lady to turn to the Lord; however the lady refused. The Tuesday news paper, had a picture on the front page showing the lady's body. My grandmother hollered when she saw the news. She stated," God kept urging me to speak with the lady. "The lady had been snatched and murdered that Monday night. I thought to myself, that could have been me. There are times people scuff at the thought of going to church or being religious, but I can say that my life was spared because of my spiritual back ground. Many of my class mates are not here today and was deceased at a young age because of their choice in life.

I continued to sew for my grandmother and others in the church while I lived with her. I still sew to this day.I also took up crocheting. I have made whole outfits in crochet. Somehow , I lost the touch of crocheting, but as I said I still sew. I believe in the process of marrying and starting a family replaced the time desire for continuing with crocheting. I have made many garments for people in my life time. I made the majority of my children's clothing, until they decided that they wanted store bought clothes. I have made drapes for churches, brides maid dresses, suits, robes and so much more. I thank God for the talent because I only took clothing I and II in high school. The rest of my knowledge for sewing was given to me. The gift was passed to my second oldest daughter for she sews beautifully. She has even showed me a few things on these new sewing machines. Her talent has gone beyond mine. She does embroidery, print to garments and HTV iron ons. She does very professional work. I am so proud of her accomplishments. She is not the only one that I am proud of; she has eight siblings and they have all made me cry with joy. I bust in excitement when I am asked of any of my children's accomplishments. I will speak more about my children in the upcoming chapters or volumes.

Volume Two
INTRODUCTION

This book is the second volume of **Come Take a Journey With Me**. It will depict highlights of my marriage. It will show the good and the bad of the marriage. Some readers, especially my children, may not like this volume of my book, because it will enlighten unpleasant aspects of our life, that is not as pleasant as one would like to read of a parent. However this is my story, and no one can express the details, except for the one who has the experience. Hopefully, as you read this, perhaps you can see yourself in this situation or someone close to you. Reading someone else's story will sometimes bring light to your own situation. I hope that it will help you see what you are doing wrong and correct it ,or you see some good that you are doing and then maybe even improve what you are doing.

I want you to know that the outcome of my marriage does not have to be your outcome. This is simply a guide to show what is good and what is not so good. I feel a person should always go into a marriage with the intention of *forever.* Marriage is not something that you take lightly. However that has to be an understanding with both parties. It is a strain on a marriage when it seems only one party is serious and the other is not.

I encourage you to put forth every effort possible to keep your marriage alive, spicy, fun and yes even challenging. Be real with yourself, there is no marriage that does not have challenges, because you are two different individuals trying to merge into one. The best thing to do is to find a common ground and work from there. But you must be real with each other. You must be patient.

To those who are not married, please take your time to really know the individual. It it easy to be on your best behavior for 3-6 months, or maybe a little longer. But most of the time a person can not put on an act for much longer. They will show their true color, and when they do please do not ignore. If it bothered you when it happened, it will continue to bother you, but it will only get worse. ***Stop*** allowing yourself to get caught up in the moment. The moment only last for awhile. It is better to break it off soon and hurt a little, than to wait, get involved deeply, have a lot at stake and then have to break up. It becomes devastating with much more hurt.

CHAPTER ONE
MY MARRIAGE LIFE

THE DYNAMICS OF THIS UNION

I finished classes in January of 1968, and graduated that June. My friend/school mate-church associate, graduated the following June. He received the baptism of the Holy Spirit on March 13th, 1969. I received the baptism of the Holy Spirit on April 25, 1969. By August 10th, 1969, we were married. We were both fresh out of school, had no clue what we wanted out of life. I do not know why we married so young, other than the fact that we were somewhat put together.(Similar to past history when marriages were arranged). Neither of us knew what we were doing, and no one sat us down, to explain the vicissitude of life. We were as green as unripe tomatoes and hard green apples. The two of us needed much counseling and healing. My husband, coming from a broken home ,with a mother that was present, but just as absent to motherhood as my mother not being present at all. At least, I had the opportunity ,of dreaming how my mother and I would have been if she was alive, but he could not change the situation with his mother. Unfortunately, we were two wounded individuals, trying to build a life together, unaware, that each had compound hurt and anguish built inside. It simulated the erosion in a chimney, just waiting for the right moment to explode. Not really knowing what caused the explosion ; only left to pick up the broken pieces time and time again.

My husband was not taught, or shown, how to love and care for someone else. All he knew was, "here go sell these pop bottles and cans and go to the store and get this." He was handed a list, of things to purchase, after he received the money from the sells. He did this time and time again; no matter the weather. This was his contribution, to help feed his mother, siblings and him. Yet he received the left overs of food, poor sleeping arrangement and clothing. He was forced, to play the role of the provider, at such a young age. The only thing in his mind was " I can not wait until I am old enough to get a job, I will make things right for me", his vow was to do for himself. And yes, he deserved that, but he was not taught that having a wife and potential family, is a great responsibility. He lacked the skills of being a good husband or father. He did not know how to care for a family, nor did he understand that there were sacrifices that he would have to make. He never considered putting his wife and family before himself. Perhaps, if he could have waited for marriage and learned a little about life. He could have watched other men, in how they worked and cared for their family. This could have alerted him, to the fact that life as he knew was much different, and maybe he could have had a different perspective on the role as a husband and father. I believe he did his best, under the circumstances, that he experienced and comprehended in his life as a child. Life as he knew, seemed to have a continuous, circulation of craters and valleys. While in the valley, it is hard to understand, that these unfortunate situations, are there to strengthen and equip you. Like David in the Bible, he was anointed to be King, but he did not receive the kingship until after he had gone through many hardships, which caused him to matured. So maturity was necessary.

Now my situation was different, but just as toxic. I was a bruised young lady that needed a lot of consoling. I felt I was born into a family that no one cared about me. My brother and I was stuck in the middle, of an endless battle. There was an older set of siblings and a younger set. So the middle set seemed invisible. My problem was ignored, as if **who cares** what bothers you. I had no mother to talk to, and on top of that, I was always told, to look at other peoples situation, and consider them instead of sulking in mine. I needed to take time to love myself and heal from my wounds. Instead, I looked to others for confirmation, which ensued a question, "am I being blessed or loved? I had to grasp the concept, that I did not need any ones approval of **me being me**. It was necessary, for me to know, that I was perfect and wonderfully made. In Genesis 1:31, God saw everything that he made, and behold, it was very good. This perception was not understood until sometime later in my life; therefore, at the time of marriage, I was expecting my husband to fill that void and become my consoler. But of course, that did not happen. His necessity for love, consoling, understanding and patients was greater than mine. In retrospect it was almost impossible for this union to flourish. I did not say **impossible, just almost,** which means it would take a lot of work and with both parties on board. My conclusion of a premature marriage is a disaster waiting to happen, a catastrophe that is not dissolved and a mystery that has no conclusion.

On a positive note, I must say, he was a great worker. Many times he would get laid off from one job, but he hustle to find another. He never became despaired and settled for less. He always pushed forward, which enabled him to gain success, by obtaining the ability to progress at an accelerated level . He was eager to learn, which was a great asset to his employer. At times he would start at entry level, but was quickly promoted and received awards. One of his greatest accomplishments, was when he became a Journeyman Machinist; however, when he became a Mechanical Engineer, working for Naval Avionics, later changing the name to Raytheon, he had reach his ultimate goal. He worked as an Engineering for over 30 years. Raytheon, along with many supervisors were blessed to have him as an employee. My husbands final position at Raytheon, was Senior Design checking Engineer where he had signing authority. When his initials were signed to a drawing the finish product was superb. He was very dedicated to his work , to his music and to his salvation. I just wished he was as dedicated to his marriage and family. Now, perhaps in his mind , he thought he was. But when you have not been shown how that works; you lack the knowledge of what to do and how it is to be done.

CHAPTER TWO
THE BEGINNING

In the beginning of our marriage I unloaded a lot of confidential information on him about me. I explained my feeling and the things I had been through. At the time, I did not realize , I was overloading him with information that he could not handle. As I previously stated, he was in a dilemma himself, therefore he was unable to comprehend the seriousness of the matter. Again, I knew of his situation, was willing to help and stand by him, even though I was not pleased with the situation, of marrying him. But he could not comprehend the dynamics of his position as a husband and future father. I, was very sensitive to the thought of once again being mistreated. I hoped that he would be more thoughtful and concern for others or me, than what he had displayed during courting, but I was wrong. I should have never expected that of him. My husband on the other hand, expected me to lose my identity, thoughts, likes and dislikes and become consumed in only what he wanted. I felt I had already lost my identity through life itself. I needed to be lifted up and encouraged. I needed to be able to sit quietly with my husband and lay my head on his shoulder or in his chest , and be assured that I was loved and he had my back. I needed to just feel like he cared. Not just a vessel for him to seek pleasure. However, he was just being released from being a substitute provider by demand, and needed time and space to just care for himself. He was not ready nor mentally willing to be responsible for any one other than himself.

He needed time to heal from the disaster that lived in. We were two individuals that had to emerge into one union, and to do that we **both** had to be willing to compromise. Unfortunately, that was not happening. But sadly we put forth an effort to have a marriage.

When I say we put forth an effort to have a marriage; we gave it a try. We started right away having a family. By our first year anniversary we were expecting a child the next month. This compound the chaos and dilemma. for we now had to make decisions for someone else. We had not yet learned how to make good decisions for ourself or each other. A lot of our ideas were not the same. His thoughts, as his role as a husband and father were nothing like I had seen and experienced. My father worked to provide for his family. He put his family first, then himself. My husband, who I will call Andy, made it plain to me that he came first in every situation then the family. It was hard for me to adjust to this type of mentality for a family structure. He had little control in setting boundaries. Either he was shy of responsibilities or going off the spectrum in handling situation that needed his attention. There was never a happy medium. His attitude was either it is done my way or no way at all. Unfortunately, that can not and will not create a healthy relationship nor a strong structural communication for rearing children.

Children need strong, sound, but relaxed boundaries that must be implemented throughout their infantry, adolescent, teenage and young adult lives. Relaxed boundaries does not mean no discipline, it only means, to know and understand each child. To know each child, and to know when the discipline should be altered, less or more, depending on the child. He was unable to comprehend or grasp this concept therefore losing the confidence and respect from some of his children. He was reared in a family , that exemplified favoritism. It was sad to know ,he was not able to break free, from this devastating and harmful parental ritual. One would think after experiencing the hurt and despair, in being a victim of such actions, that you would not incur this behavior on others. Sadly, he visited these behaviors on his eight children; he demonstrated favoritism with the second oldest son. I tried appealing to him, the sensitive nature of this matter, it was to no avail. Many unrested feelings developed from this action. To this day, I can see little tolerance toward this son from some of his siblings. Unfortunately, it was not his fault nor theirs, but never the less, the dissension exists.

Sometimes in discipline the children, his punishment was beyond comprehension. I had a hard time controlling my self, when he discipline them, because I felt his actions had surpass the disciplinary stage and was leaning towards child abuse; in which I did not want to be tanted with this label. We were taught that when one parent is disciplining the children the other parent should not interfere. I tried that many times by going in a different room or outside, but there were times I had to intervene. I recall an incident; my oldest son was acting out in his class. His teacher decided to call his dad at his place of employment, in which I had already noted in their school records, not to do, because I was home and could have handled the situation, but she was quite upset, so she took matters in her own hand and made that call. Well needless to say the consequences for that son was devastating. The child was made to fill the tub with hot water, not scawlding hot, and then soak in the water. After he soaked a bit ,his dad beat him with a belt that seemed eternal. Then his dad told him to get out of the tub, dry off. His dad's next words sent me in a whirlwind. He told him, " now I am just getting ready to beat you." I could not stand to hear another round of licks given to that child. This was a time when I had to intervene. I ran in that bathroom like lightening. **I, "said if you hit him one more time , you will have to beat me too, and you know that is not going to happen." At the same time our oldest child ran to the door and just started hollering, "STOP IT DADDY,STOP IT."** So you can imagine the chaos at that moment. But he had to be stopped. Now, this same teacher called crying the next day, when she saw the results of the child's punishment. *Had I not been,* a Christian woman, this lady would have had words catapulting to her that she had never heard before. But thank God , he held my tongue. She explained that she could have called Child Protective Service, but she felt she was at fault. I said, "yes, you are at fault, because, it is in my children's records to call me".

My oldest son seem to disturb his father a great deal. He was a little slower to catch on to things; not like his brother who was just 11 months his junior, who quickly surpassed him in developmental stages, and in School. This should have never been a problem; all children have their own pace in development. No child should be compared to another child. Somehow, this caused undo discipline to the older son. This was very disturbing to me, and it heightened the mother protection mold. I knew all to well the feeling of being mistreated. Slow development creates a complex within itself, it should not increase anxiety, because of mistreatment from misinterpreted ideas of others. Many times his punishment was missing dinner. I disagreed with using essential necessities for punishment such as sending a child to bed without dinner, or not having anything to eat all day. I would sneak food to my son after his father had gone to bed or left the house. That may not have been the right thing to do, but as a mother I could not stand to see them go to bed without food.

Another example of our division with discipline was, a time when Andy disciplined my oldest daughter unprovoked and untimely. I was 6 or 7 months pregnant with our 8th child. It was on a Saturday . I can not recall if Andy was at work or just out. The majority of his Saturdays were spent outside of the home. Very few of those Saturdays were for work. It was in the evening, because the children had already eaten dinner. I Had cleaned the house and had gotten the children's clothes prepared for Sunday. My daughter and her cousin, 7 & 8 respectively, who visited our home frequently, were washing ribbons for their hair for Sunday. I was tired so I allowed them to wash the ribbons themselves. I figured I would have to mop up a little water, but that was ok. I was sitting in a chair next to the kitchen where the girls were. I am watching them, and yes they were making a little mess with water on the floor. I was waiting until they were done to mop up their spill. In the meantime Andy came home, saw the water on the floor and went ballistic. He ordered the child to mop the entire kitchen; which was unnecessary, because the entire kitchen was not affected, only the spot in front of the sink. In that day we had big heavy mops. The mop was heavy for me to handle , less lone a 7 year old child. I explained that she could not handle that mop and I was going to mop up the spill once they were done. I enraged him more by making that statement. I went into the bathroom to rinse the mop. While I was ringing out the mop, I heard this commotion in the kitchen, He had begin to beat her with his belt all across her back. I forgot I still had the mop in my hand until I used it on him to stop him from beating the child. It was not until, **he** started to holler that I realized what I was doing.

By then, the damage was done. My daughter stop crying, and both she and her cousin were standing there eyes big as quarters and mouth opened wide. I do not know if they were scared, surprised or both. I was exhausted, puzzled and in disbelief of what had just happened.

How could a perfect day turn into a disaster within minutes?
Why did that make him so upset?
Did he not see me sitting there?

I **was** a parent , at home all day with the children. Managed to clean the house, fix dinner and get prepared for Sunday. What made him think that I was not capable of handling this situation. Actually, I did not see a problem. If there was a need to be upset about the water on the floor; certainly that should have been me. I am the one who cleaned the house. Out of respect to me, his wife, he should have enquire of me about the water. I could have explained what they were doing and that I was going to handle the mess. Simple as that. In stead I was disciplined by the leaders at church. For the wife is supposed to be subject to her husband. Although I think this concept is taken to extreme. If I saw my husband trying to cut a cilds throat; do I allow it , trying to be submissive or do I try and stop him? You can be assured that I would do everything in my power to stop him. I am not saying that Andy would have gone to that extreme; I am just letting you know that if the situation warranted intervention. I would navigate the intervention.

When you experience watching your father sacrifice and not have things for himself, in order that his family may have not only the necessities, but also things such as Iife and health insurances, change of underwear and clothing for school as well as church. He made sure his sons clothes were pressed and ready for church and that they were looking as decent as he. Although he left the welfare of his daughters in the hands of the wife, he provided what was needed. My father very seldom missed having Sunday dinner with the family and during the week, if he was not present for dinner, the family was allowed to eat without him. We always made sure there was food enough for him. The family was not allowed to eat dinner before Andy; even if he decided that he was not coming home at his usual time. I had to pacify crying hungry children, while Andy did God knows what. I thought what I saw my father do, was standard practices. I was appalled when I learned that these things were not an interest to Andy. He was not having health or life insurance deducted from his earnings. His statement to me was, "I will only provide a place to live for the family, feed and clothe them, as long as I live. I do not care what happens to the family when I am dead."

WHAT???

Who does that?

Don't you care for your family?

Well, I was not going to stand silent on this matter. So I stepped in, and did, what most men say of their wives, I became a nagging wife until finally he gave in and purchased life and health insurance which was deducted from is earnings. Of course, it was not in weeks or months, but it did happen. I became like the widow in Luke 18: 1-8, The judge was not afraid of anyone, so he denied the widow of justice many times; but because of the widows persistence the judge granted the petition of the widow less she worry him. My persistence and yes, you can say nagging, allowed the children to be covered in insurance and I was able to **breath**. You see, I am glad I was persistent in Andy getting health insurance especially. I had two children that had asthma, one bitten by a dog and one child to get hit by an ice-cream truck.

Another thing I felt was distasteful, was the matter of Andy ,telling everything that went on in our home; no matter what, he exposed it. If a child misbehaved in school ,to someone having a problem with bed wetting, to his daughters coming into womanhood it was exposed. There was no privicy ; even to the fact of him exposing our personal business to everyone he talked to . Our bedroom life might as well have been on TV , because he felt it necessary to talk about it even to our sons. I tried to explain to him, that these circumstances, are not things that you expose of your family. I would ask him, " are these people that you expose your family to, exposing their family?" Of course not, but he was so engrossed in what he was saying, that he was unaware of the response he received. I would be the one that received the response of how embarrassed they were. Their comment would be, "why would he expose his family like that? I would never talk about my family like this". His comment would be, "well they should not do things if they do not want it exposed".

What?

For real?

There was a time I was having medical conditions; I had to have surgery. Andy was telling many of the church members what type of surgery and why I had the surgery. I was so embarrassed. It was hard for me to go back to church after my recovery. There was this constant exposure of our family life, that eventually I had had enough, so I went to a different assembly. Unfortunately this magnified the separation of our family. We drove two separate vehicles, because we could not all fit in one; therefore when I changed assemblies that meant those that rode with me changed too. When I say that it magnified the separation; there was a distinct separation between the males and females in our home. The males where made to feel that they were on a higher level than the females. The statement was made, The girls do not really matter because they will get married and their husband will take care of them. **Wrong,** females are not, second class citizens, that have to depend on someone to make a success of life, in order for them to enjoy life. The males were given accolades in their academic successes, but the females were just snubbed and said that is nice. I took it upon myself to encourage my daughters to be the best they could be ." I do not want you to depend on anyone for your success. You can become successful on your own". Thank goodness they comprehended and succeeded. Yes they were, or are married; however their success did not or do not come from their spouses. They achieved goals before and after marriage.

CHAPTER THREE
WARNING SIGNS

Signs can be missed during courting or dating stages, because you did not date long enough. We often miss or ignore, tell - tell signs of the characteristics of a partner to be, because we are living in the moment. Looking all google eyed and caught up in a new experience. But, I serve notice, that the moment will not last. You need to observe that individual, beyond, the few months that everything is **peachy dandy**. Mature adults, that is courting, will seek as much information about that person as possible. It is imperative that you discuss both parties' likes and dislikes. You discuss your outlooks on disciplinary measures, facts of life and both perceptions of the different aspects of life. You make sure you are compatible, and if your differences can be compromised, or come to a peaceful agreement. These things are very important to a successful long term union. Now mind you we did talk about this some but not to the fullest extent. We talked about it enough that I knew I did not like his idea of disciplinary nor his outlook on becoming a husband and father.

Why did I go through with the marriage? It had a lot to do with the way I was taught, insecurities and little self worth that complicated matters. As I stated earlier I was wounded from rejection. Losing my mom at an early age, having a stepmom that was not fond of me and having to step back for every unfortunate person, that my grandmother fostered or took in. Little did my grandmother know that the very ones she was trying to help, were causing problems and dissention between my grandmother, my brother, and me. They would make trouble with us, then report to my grandmother the opposite of what really happen . Her decision to defuse situations seemed to lean towards the guest. She would pull us aside and say, "I know it is hard, but they will not be here for long; just give them a break". In every circumstance your feelings did not seem to matter. It was always to prefer other's feeling over yours. I know, none of these situations were planned, nor were they meant to belittle , uproot or harm me, but it did.

However, living with my grandmother was more relaxing and peaceful. The atmosphere was just different. Although there was always someone living with her besides my brother and me; she had control over how things would be. There was not a lot to do as children, but we knew how to go out and create our fun. The food was not rationed, not that it was a bad thing, but it was fewer mouths to feed. No one called us greedy, nor were we always threatened with ,"I going to tell your dad when he gets home". There was very little discipline needed. First of all, we knew we would get in grave trouble with our father, if he found out we were misbehaving and secondly, we did not want to be sent back home. So we came in at a decent time, we were obedient, mind our manners and distance ourselves from the adults.

Not only was she my grandmother; she was my spiritual guidance; she was the founder and pastor of Believer's In Christ Tabernacle. So she had a great influence over me and the other parishioners. Being a female she added a motherly atmosphere to her ministry causing many to gravitate to her more than normal. I for one, took her word as gospel. During our courtship it was more my grandmother and Andy's mother that seemed to be getting the greater enjoyment out of biblical scriptures and quoted phrases . My fiancé' and I went along for the ride. Now I do not know how he was excepting the scriptures quoted, but they were just that to me, scriptures quoted. To give an example of a scriptures, in(Ruth 1) it pertains to Naomi, and Ruth. Naomi was Ruth's mother-in-law. After the passing of both her husband and sons, Naomi expressed to both Ruth and the other daughter-in-law, that it was best for them to go back to their own home town. The expression that was quoted often was, Ruth's reply," where you go I go, where you lay I lay; your God will be my God". Now that sound good and the words are powerful, but did I really take that to heart? Was that my sentiment? Not at all, but like I said I was living in the moment and yes I excepted the proposal. This is where I made the biggest mistake of my life. I should not have allowed fear to misguide me. I was afraid of hurting the young man's feelings. Afraid of what my grandmother would have said or thought. Afraid of the whispers," hummm, I guess she thinks she is better than him". How dumb of me.

Before and after the proposal there was little courtship during the engagement and that entailed someone always tagging along. So when I expressed that I did not like his ideas and I did not want to marry him; the words of Ruth that I did not say, neither did I express that this was my sentiment was excepted as a promise that I was not allowed to break. To break an engagement was strongly disapproved by the church. The only approved excuse was if either of the two broke the promise by being unfaithful. So when my pastor/ grandmother stated that you could not break a promise she meant that. You never wanted to get on her bad side. It would be like you stepped into the Artic Circle, causing the space between you and her to freeze. Or like a duck sitting in the middle of a pond, when suddenly the temperature drops to 10 below and the pond freezes over with the poor duck. So unfortunately I had no choice at that time but to go forward with the marriage. One would say why not just break the engagement and go to another assembly. It was not that simple. You could not go to another church and be a member unless the previous pastor sent a good standing letter to the present pastor........... I felt I was entrapped in a situation that was impossible to break free . So I chose to give it my best. After all he was tall and handsome , he could play an organ and as I mention before, he could be loads of fun at times. Andy and I were both silly and loved to laugh. There were times we would just look at each other and burst into laughter especially if a situation warranted humor. We often laughed at situations with the children growing up that some people may have believe as parents ; warranted a sturn and firm discipline. Discipline came later after we had settled from an exuberant laugh. Both of us had hardy laughs; so when matters became funny there was a roar of laughter. Andy laughed so hard that he would bang on the table if we were at the table , or stump the floor if we were sitting elsewhere. We had many church affiliates and acquaintances, but few actual true friends. We would often come together for fellowship to eat, talk and play games. The noise from our laughter would permeate the house; but when games began , I believe the neighbors on both sides could hear the roaring sounds of loudness and laughter. There were times we would go out for dinner with friends and once again laughter was hardy. I am glad we were never asked to leave the restaurant, but we did get a few stares and glares; some with approval and others not. Andy was a peculiar guy. His mannerism and characteristics were different from most individuals which made him unique but strange. He could humor you by his actions or deeds unintended. At times his expressions were hilarious and yet other times annoying. We had many ups and downs, but we gave it twenty one years, before I finally outgrew his level of maturity. It was time for me to move on with many oppositions. By then I was stronger, had self confidence and was determine not to allow gossip to deter me.

CHAPTER FOUR

CHILDREN

In this union we had nine children. Five sons and four daughters. My oldest, Monica, was a daughter, she was warm, friendly and never met a stranger, but she was a sassy little toddler; who kept us laughing. She thought she was the second mother in the house. Actually more outside the house. She would always fight her siblings battles, even if the sibling had started the battle. It did not matter. She was there to settle the matter, everybody was aware of her , so they shyed away when her presence was near. My oldest son, loved to tease the younger siblings. He would have them running to me crying for him to leave them alone. One time, he push his brother, the one next to the baby, to the point that all I heard was a growl, and next thing I saw, was that child charging toward his brother like a bull charge to battle. I could not stop laughing. Sabastian was quiet and to himself , so it was really funny to see him react in this manner. My second oldest son, was funny. He was smart as he could be, but very hyper. I would always say," boy if you don't go sit down. "The second daughter, Tabitha was quiet and shy, but loved to sing. The third son, was my hungry child. He would stand at the stove while I was cooking impatiently asking "is it done yet". I would have to order him to go sit down. Now my third and fourth daughters were twins. Totally unexpected, but a joy to our entire church community. I had to turn some church goers away from wanting to keep "the twins" overnight. The fourth son was the one I mentioned that bull headed his older brother. The fifth and final son and child was my baby. He was my little preacher and prayer warrior.

Now to make this more personable, I am going to give each child a name, that is not the original name, to make it easier to keep up with each child. I will call my oldest daughter, Monica. The oldest son will be Wayne, the second oldest son Aurthur, the second oldest daughter Tabitha, the middle son which is the third, Geoffrey, the twins, Jolene and Janae, the fourth son Sabastian and the last and final son and child, Ardale. Wow! I hope I can remember those names myself. My children will probably say "where did you pull those names, out of the sky"? I will just laugh and say that it was the first name to come to me from their original names. Now this is going to be a ride. Fasten your seat belts. I will give a little excerpt of each child's book of life. I will give little bits and pieces of each child's funny moments ,sincere moments and accomplishments. Not a lot, just enough, for you to get a picture of their character.

Monica was the child that kept you on your toes; she was a character. She being the first born of our union and the first born great granddaughter; I don't have to tell you that she was spoiled. Monica was in a household of adults. In the beginning of our marriage we lived with my grandmother, my great aunt, grandmother's sister and an adopted teenage girl, so she learned and matured very quickly. At six months old she was in her bed sitting up playing, my brother came over to see us and began to teasingly pick with Monica. To our surprise she told him to get out of here. We were all stunned because first we did not know she could talk nor understood what she said. Another time, this same brother of mine, was teasing her and she said a curse word that we did not know she knew because know one in the house cursed. Unfortunately, unbeknownst to us, the adopted teenager, had been teaching her to say this word. Again we were shocked. When it came time to chastise her, **corporal punishment**, which was legal in our time, neither her father nor I wanted to administer that. We knew that by the time we were done we would have received the most licks. So,we would debate, on who's turn it was to deliver. fortunate for her, the punishment was canceled. Monica is frantically afraid of dogs. One time I had taken her to the store. I was sitting in the car waiting on her to return. It was in the spring so while sitting in the car I had the windows rolled half way down. Upon returning she heard a dog. Monica took off running to the car and instead, of opening the door to get in, she jumped through the half rolled window. My mouth flew open, because I just knew she was going to kill herself. Thank God he protected her. To this day I do not know how she did that. When she jumped in ,she slid her little self in the seat as if she had opened the door and got in. After I caught my breath and saw she was okay, we both laughed so hard for awhile. Another momentum moment was when she faked a kidnap. I will never forget. For some reason, she thought I was taking the side of her brother, in a dispute. She thought, if I took his side, I no longer loved her. So, she planned a big surprise for us all. I came home from work one day. The chairs in the living room were turned over and other things in disarray. Then there was the **note!** It was like a ransom note; **"if you want to see your child again,"** and of course the amount of money. I can not remember how much money was in the note(10,000-20,000), but I should have known that the amount asked, no real kidnapper would do. But, I went into a panic, called her father, all the while crying and hollering,

"Oh my God !!

Why ?

Who would do such a thing?"

By the time Andy got home he was in a frenzy. He read the note and then said, **"we don't have this kind of money. Where are we going to get it ."** It took a bit for it to really sink in. I retrieved the letter and read it again. That is when it resonated in me that this did not make sense. I immediately called her and said, " get out here right now." And, " **what to our wondering eyes did appear? Monica stepped out of the coat closet."** Her father and I were too weak to chastise her at the moment. The exhaustion from the whole ordeal left us drained**.** All we could say was," **Why"?** We ordered her to go to her room. Only to find out a day or two later, the reason she pulled such a shananigan. Monica grew up to be a beautiful young lady who served her country through the institution of The National Guards. In her tenure she was able to go over seas to different countries. She was stationed in Manheim, Germany-Military finance, milpay and accounting. Camp Bondsteel, Kosovo-Military finance, milpay and accounting. She was able to go to New Delhi, India through her employment with Conseco, to train Excel services associates, on insurance premium accounting. Monica received her Bachelors: in Business Management., Masters in Organizational Management and Doctorate in Leadership and Organizational Change. She has given me two beautiful granddaughters, four great grandsons and six great granddaughters. She is now teaching a special curriculum of Business Administration to Middle School and College students. Monica has excepted her calling in the Ministry of God, she has been ordained under the New Wineskin Ministries under the tutelage of Doctor Mark Brown Sr. She has delivered several inspiring sermons and teachings.

Wayne, who loved to tease the younger siblings; explained to me later that he was trying to toughen them to be men. Being the oldest boy, he too, like my daughter, took it upon himself to protect the younger boys. If he thought someone was bullying them he stepped in to defuse the situation. Wayne was the son that I often had to go around his father's chastisement and give him food or just to make sure he was alright. He was quiet and did not require a lot of attention, but somehow seemed to be passed over by his father. He unlike Monica, would except his punishment and would go on as if nothing happened. Wayne was one of my good eaters. I could get him to try new foods before some of his siblings. Wayne would keep his class mates laughing in school which lead to him receiving a terrible beating in which I found myself intervening, because it was too harsh. Wayne used the school as his space to vent his frustration because home was too monitored and suffocating. He had all these younger siblings crowding his space and the brother that was closet to him was always gone. So he became the class jokester keeping the class lively and making his mates laugh. One thing that Wayne and his brother Geoffrey did, that their father nor I knew anything about, until years later , was while they were on their paper route they would pretend they were so hungry. The neighborhood knew about the Mimms with so many children. So they would feel sorry for them and give them food to eat. Now mind you, they had just eaten dinner. They were growing boys and the food seem to go to their feet. Then neighbors were really neighbors. They did not mind helping you if you were in need. At Christmas time Wayne and his brothers that had paper routes would receive nice monetary gifts from their customers. I remember once when Wayne was about sixteen or maybe seventeen, one of the hairstyles for guys was with a braided tail. Oh boy, Wayne and his father had many disputes about his hair. His father was determined that he was going to cut it, but Wayne was just as determine he was not going to cut it. One day I was taken by surprise because it actually became a tussle between the two of them. I felt bad for both of them; my son had never done anything like that and his father, well lets just say, I felt bad for him. Wayne and his father severed their differences and Wayne was his father's barber until he passed away. Wayne went to school for barbering and now owns his own barber shop. He is doing well for himself. Unfortunately he has not given me any grandchildren.

Arthur, the third child was so funny. He was smart as he could be, but very energetic. I would always say," boy if you don't go sit down." He would sit down for a bit, but not for long. It was not that he would make excessive noise; but it was the constant movement. He loved to laugh. When something funny happened, his eyes would widen, he would rub his hands together and he would roar with laughter. He was very good at assisting his older brother with daily essentials. One day I was getting the children ready to go, probably to church. I asked him to help his brother get ready. He was three and Wayne was four. He sensed that his brother was slow and therefore, received more attention. Now Arthur, spoke very well, but on this particular day, he asked me, **" you wa me to wa hi fa wi waf wag?" I turned and looked at him, I said, "boy if you don't stop that and talk right. What is wrong with you?"** Later after getting everybody settled, I just chuckled to myself. Unfortunately, he was separated from his siblings most of the time, because his father chose him, to be his running buddy; even at a young age. While in high School he was in Counter Points and during his tenure at Wabash he was in the Glee Club; which gave him great experience in singing and traveling to different states to perform. Arthur was the first child to leave home for college. He went to Wabash College in Crawfordsville, IN to do undergrad studies; then returned home to attend IUPUI University for his Masters, IU for his Doctorate and then to Michigan for Residency. He is a successful Physiatrist with his own practice. He has increased our family with his wife and two beautiful daughters. The oldest is attending Butler University in undergrad studies. While there she is the second violinist in orchestra. The second is a Junior in High School. Arthur has excepted his ministerial calling and has delivered several inspiring sermons and teachings. He has been Ordained through the New Wineskin Ministries under the tutelage of Bishop Byron Johnson.

My fourth child was a daughter. Tabitha was shy at times, but innocently bold. When she was a toddler she would get a song and would sing it seemingly endlessly. My grandfather loved to hear her sing. he would say, " come here little girly, sing grandpa a song." One of her favorite songs was, "Lord I know you've been so good." **of course she wouldn't say Lord, it was Nord, I know do been toe good."** She loved her older sister so much that she would do what ever she told her to do. One particular time she and Monica were going on a trip with my grand mother. There was a cousin that normally went with them on trips, but this particular time another little girl was going. This perturbed Monica, so when the other girl boarded the RV, Monica told Tabitha to slap the girl. And of course, she did. When I asked her why, she did that, she shrugged her shoulders and said Monica told me to. Now, she was only three when this happened. One other time the family went to dinner with a friend of the family.

We were eating and conversating, when it was mentioned, that someone at the table was really shoving their food down. Tabitha raised her head from her plate and said, "**uumhum just like a hungry bastard,**" and continued to eat. Now, this was not a word that was used in our household. So, once her father, our friend , I and older siblings got over the **shock,** we burst into laughter. I did not think we would ever stop. But she never gave any indication that maybe that was not the word to use in front of her parents. That is what made it more hilarious. When Tabitha was a baby and toddler; she would not let me out of her sight. She was so cute which drew others to make comment or speak to her. She was not having that. Tabitha would grab hold to my dress, for dear life and began to cry if the person lingered to long in front of her. She has always been a loner. I believe it would have been different if she and Monica were closer in age. Tabitha is the daughter I spoke of earlier about an excellent seamstress and Monogram Designer. Tabitha went to IUPUI and received an Bachelor Degree in Engineering . She is currently working at Crane Naval Base as an Engineer. She has blessed me with three handsome grandsons and a beautiful granddaughter. Her eldest son is also an Engineer who works at Crane. The next son is a Correctional Officer in Plainfield . He is currently seeking his degree. The third son is also currently in school for his degree. The daughter is in her last year of a four undergrad Studies.

My fifth child was a son. He is considered the middle child. Geoffrey seemed to play out all the stigma plagued to being a middle child. But not at first. He loved to eat and was the first to always ask if the food was done. When he came home from school , the first thing he would check, was to see if food was being prepared. If not that meant dinner would be served later. He was gifted in finance. At a young age he would figure how to make money. He would make little trinkets from paper and sell them to his classmates. At seven he had a paper route and with his pay he would purchase candy from the wholesale store and sell that . He had three of his siblings in business for him, selling the candy at school. They did well until they were caught. This did not stop him because they sold the candy in the neighborhood. Geoffrey was the other son whom along with his older brother made the neighbor's think they did not have enough food to eat. (The little stinkers, Lol) I remember the time when he was hit by a car, running to get to the ice cream truck. That was a scary moment. All I could think of was my child was dead, but before I could get out of the door, he jumped up still trying to get to that truck. **Thank God,** the x rays showed no broken bones. However, he suffered a lot with his stomach after the accident. I spent many nights up with him, Praying and giving him medicine. Thankfully the pain subsided. To this day I am not aware of him having any stomach problems. Geoffrey is another child that has received a Bachelor Degree in Engineer. He worked at Allison for years and took an early retirement in 2020. He has his own Tax company and is doing very well. He and his wife has blessed me with eight grandchildren. (I say **blessed me**, because their father has passed on). Four of each just as handsome and beautiful as they can be.

After all the children I had already; I was surprised with a set of twins. Jolene and Janae. These girls were the talk of our church community. They were the first twins in the church. Andy and I were taken back when we heard the news. It was so unexpected to me that, after the doctor had delivered the first child and said "I feel an arm" upon explaining it to me; I went balistic thinking he had broke my baby's arm. Although I had already seen the baby. It still did not register until I was ordered to be put to sleep. **OH NO SIR, not until you tell me what is happening.** He said" you have another baby ma'am". As I was going out, all I could do is hold up two fingers. My thought was this pregnancy was going to make my sixth child, what am I going to do with seven now?

Jolene was the oldest of the two. Her face was a cute little round circle. Although she weighed five ounce more than her sister, she was the shortest. Many could not tell them apart; though they had their own membrane sac fused together. Jolene was the feisty one. She would let you know if she did not like something. I think at first when the two were toddlers, Jolene may have felt it was not fair she had to share everything with her sister. I did not know until later of course that she felt this way. Maybe I would not have dressed them alike. Perhaps I could have had the same style but different colors. I adored them dressed alike. I recall making them a peach and white and a red and white dresses. They were both adorable, but I think they and I loved the peach and white best. Jolene and Janea were both small built; yet they were the bossiest little ladies. They tried their best to make their brothers behave and complete the chores assigned to them. Of course it was to no avail. The boys would only push them out of the room or away from them. This seemed disastrous to the twins; they were only trying to help. The next step was running to me crying. Only to hear mommy say," honey, they are too big for you , just leave them alone." Eventually, when I stepped in to chastise all of them for not completing their chores; I could hear the little voices saying," see I told you, now you made all of us get into trouble." Even though, Jolene thought, Janea was in her way; because they shared everything, The two are now best friends. Jolene is now a Licensed Marriage and Family Therapist, LMFT. She did her undergrad studies at IUPUI,graduating with a Communication Degree with an emphasis on Family Communication. She attended Christian Theological Seminary to complete a degree in Marriage and Family Therapy. She now has her own private practice, Healing Paths Family Counseling, LLC. Jolene's cliental consist of individuals, families and couples that need assistance in sustaining healthy lives. Jolene and her husband, has blessed me with three beautiful granddaughters. The oldest daughter is already showing signs of entrepreneurship.

Janae is the youngest of her twin. She had this small oval face, which made the distinguished feature between the two, plus she was a half an inch longer than Jolene. The two of them was small enough to fit in the side drawer of a dresser. This was their bassinet, when they visited a particular church member. This member thought it was darling, to be able to put two drawers side by side on the coffee table, for the twins to sleep. The few nights Jolene and Janae stayed with this member, was the only nights I was able to rest. Of course I did not let the girls stay much; since they were small infants. Janae's personality was slightly different from Jolene. She was and is the one who chooses her words carefully when expressing her dislikes. **Stop!**, don't get me wrong, she is assertive when necessary. Janae and Jolene were the first that I saw to do choreography during programs sponsored by the two. It was beautiful to see them move gracefully with the music. They also taught a choir how to perform choreography in plays and performances,(this did not surprise me, for they were always making up stories and plays when they were young) which they were the producers and directors. It saddened me when they stopped performing, but they both chose to further their education in their respective careers. Janae did her undergrad studies at IUPUI, continue studies at Indiana Wesleyan University for her Masters of education and then on to Northcentral University for a MBA, Masters in Business Administration. She taught Public School for twelve years, and a Virtual Teacher for four. Her current position; is a Student Engagement and a Relationship Coach. Janae, along with her husband has blessed me with a handsome grandson and beautiful granddaughter. Janae's son will most definitely be an entrepreneur. He has taken up photography and is showing excellent skills.

Sabastian is next to the baby. He is just a year younger than the twins. He was always quite and to himself. I would go to him, to see if there was anything bothering him. He would give me a half smile and say, "no ma'am, I am fine." I would leave him alone. I remember being like that, but most of the time mine was because of insecurity. Other times I would sense that he was bothered about something so I would not give him a chance to brush me off. I would tell him I know you are bothered about something. Come on talk to me. Seeing that he was sensitive about the matter; I would assure him it was ok, he could talk to me. This is what I meant, when I said you have to know your children. Sabastian was blessed with a voice like some of his siblings; howevery his siblings talent was not discovered until later. We discovered Sabastian's talent to sing because he would be the only one that stayed around the piano and sing while Andy played. The others would ease away until Sabastian would be the last one there. Being a lot like me, he did not have the heart to leave Andy at the piano bangging on the keys and stamping his feet on the floor. Sabastian ended up singing solos many times during service by the request of his father. Soon he was known as the little Mimms singer. Like Arthur, Sabastian was in Counter Points and performed at different events. He also went to Walbash for his undergrad. He then to IU for Residency for five years, and then IU North Hospital for a Bariatric and Laparoscopic fellowship. He worked at Community Hospital and then to Wabash Hospital as Chief Surgent before opening his own practice. He has Three handsome sons and one beautiful daughter.

Now, it comes to my baby, Ardale. As I mentioned this little fellow was my preacher and prayer warrior. He was always going around preaching. He would really hack, clap his hands and stomp his little feet. I just knew he would end up being a minister. I really have not dismissed this thought as of yet; for God works in mysterious ways. What really impressed me about Ardale, and his ministerial passion, at the time, he was 30 months old. I was getting ready for hysterectomy surgery. I called all the children in the room and explained to them that I would be in the hospital for about a week. I explained I was having surgery, gave them all instructions in what to do while I would be away. After I was done little Ardale spoke up and asked if I wanted him to pray for me. I was shocked but gladly excepted. Ardale prayed like he was a big person. Believe it or not, my nerves were settled after he prayed. The rest his history, for here I am writing this memoir. Ardale always suffered from asthma. His attacks could get serious, but never chronic. I have to thank God for that. Wayne always thought I was babying Ardale, But I was being cautious with him because of his asthma. Asthma is tricky, one moment you could be fine and the next minute you could be sick as a dog. This has happened many times, to the point that his dad thought he was faking an attack.

I know, because I suffered from it all my life. I missed a lot because I was not able to do much exertion ,because I would be sick. So I was nerves for him. Many nights I was up with him suffering from asthma. One thing funny that Ardale did , which shocked me. He was about seven or eight; he and his brothers where out in the back yard playing some kind of ball. Their dad came home and began to reprimand them for playing ball. Andy was quiet strict about certain things. So, he was really laying into them. All of a sudden Ardale shouted out ,"we are going to play our ball here." The room was quite for about a space of 10 seconds. Then Andy reached over and slapped Ardale. This time it was about five seconds and Ardale and every else burst into laughter, except Andy. He turned and went into his room. Ardale has grown to be a handsome young man that went to Perdue University for his Bachelor of Science in Chemistry. He did research with tobacco moths at IUPUI and received his Doctorate of Pharmaceutical Sciences at Howard University. He has four handsome sons with two of them being twins.

I told you it would be a ride. I hope you enjoyed it. Large families are often bullied , victims of cruel jokes and poked at. But as you can see these children, teens, young adults and now adults have dissected the stigma, that large families are state liabilities and menace to society. Well it seems that all nine Of my children are assets to society. Not as predicted what they would be, but they made their own predictions and fulfilled them. I must say I am so proud of all of them . I could not have asked for a better set of children. I must say I was blessed Of God . This reminds me of a statement my maternal grandmother told me . When I told her that I did not want to marry; she asked me to do it for her and my children and I would be blessed. I must say that what she said has come to pass. This was a blind walk. I did not see that nor did I feel that . While I was in the marriage it did not feel like a blessing. It almost felt like the opposite. As a matter of fact ; my whole life was switched from what I had planned for it to be. I wanted to go to college, become a Certified Public Accountant and live a comfortable life. As I stated earlier, I was not planning on having children. I stated that I did not know if I would know how to rear up children and if I would know how to love them. I am so grateful that my plans were turned upside down. To God be the Glory.

VOLUME THREE
INTRODUCTION OF MY CHURCH LIFE

This is going to be an interesting topic. It is the third and final chapter of The Journey Of My Life. I would like to enlightened the term or stigma of" The Preacher Kid." Yes you have heard that the preacher's kid is the worst in the church. First I am going to change the preacher's kid to preacher's child or children. You see humans do not rear kids; for kids are species of animals such as goats. I do not know how this term became associated with humans, but I despise the association. Therefore I will not speak of preacher's kids , but rather preacher's children. I want to speak from a preacher's child perspective. Although I realize and have witness how unruly some children can be that have parents or grandparents as ministers. I want to appeal to the sensitivity of this matter. Not all children that are preacher's children follow the order of this stigma. You see , before you judge someone you need to walk a mile in their shoes. Most of the time, you are labeled a problem child, long before you are old enough, to portrayed any symptoms of what is said, of one being a preacher's child. What has been the greatest oversight of this topic is; preacher's children are expected to live like angels, when no one on earth lives like angels. So, from the beginning the children have been placed in an unfairly predicament that no one can fulfill the expectations. I will speak of things that I experienced being a preacher's child two times over. I will highlight certain events that I deem necessary to elaborate.

My Church Experience

I was reared in church. As I mention in the previous chapters and volumes, my maternal grandmother(Pastor Brown) was the Founder and Pastor of Believer's IN Christ Tabernacle. My father for a long time was a Deacon, and then became the

Head Deacon. While Pastor Brown was sick my father was the Interim Pastor. When Pastor Brown passed away, my father became the pastor. As far back that I can remember I was in church the majority of the time. We had some type of service Monday thru Friday. Sundays were a full day. There was Sunday School, Morning service , and night service. Every now and then we had Sunday afternoon service. Our morning services resembles nothing like services of today. Morning service started at 10:30 and may go until 1:00 or 2:00 o'clock. If the spirit of the Lord was heavy in the sanctuary the service may last longer. I can remember as young as five or six having church members picking with me . I could be with a group of children my age, just laughing and talking and someone would come up and accuse us of doing something that we were not doing. They would tell the group, God is going to get you, standing here talking and making fun of someone. Then they would look at me and say, "you ought to be ashamed of yourself, you are the pastor's granddaughter." Why should I have been treated any different. What difference did that make, who I was kine to. By the way we were not talking about anyone. Just child conversation, and something was said that was funny.

My father was not aware that people that called themselves Holy, was not as holy as he thought. If an adult said we had misbehaved, then he would not question the source. We would get into trouble whether we did what we were accused of or not. My siblings and I often discussed how discouraging it was to always be targeted. In Sunday School class, when it was time to collect offering, I would be singled out. Marcia I know you have offering. I know your grandmother gave you offering. Why would you think that? I did not come from my grandmother's I came from home. I also had other children pick with me. They thought ,I thought , I was better than they were. Why would I think that? I recall a particular Sunday, afterSunday School, a group of girls who were considered rough girls, cornered me in the vestibule and was threatening to beat me up. I had not said anything to or about these girl. They just wanted to fight me because they had this notion that I felt as if I was superior to them. Maybe it was their conscience that was bothering them. I was a church girl and though they attended Sunday School, they were not considered a church girl. They made statements as to how I dressed. "Who do you think you are?" As I stood there and observed

each of them; there was no way I was going to back down, and there was no way I could fight them all. I mustard up enough of courage and said,"get away from me, I am not afraid of you." Of course when I raised my voice, It drew attention, which made the girls back up. If only, the girls knew how afraid I was, they would have bullied me. Thank goodness I called their bluff and they never approached me again. I had a coat , my grandmother purchased for me. It was a calf lenght fox. I loved that fur coat . After that episode with the girls, I would not wear the coat unless I was going somewhere with my grandmother. I did not want the other children to think, as I mentioned before, that I felt superior to them.

In my twenties, I became a Sunday School Teacher. I loved teaching the youth. During my tenure in teaching there were several discrepancies; I would start with a class and in midstream of teaching, that class would be removed and I would get a different set of students. Usually it was closer to Sunday School review time, where each class would have to present before the whole Sunday School, what they had learned. This made it difficult to bring the class up to par for a smooth review. Teaching the classes in the beginning was always challenging. You had some students that was talkative, then you had those that was quiet and barely participated in the activities. My joy and satisfaction was when I was able to win over the quiet and reserved students. To see them began to interact with the other students ,answer questions and become excited ,I was overwhelmed with joy. I felt my mission was accomplished. The joyfulness of accomplishment did not last for long. There was always someone confronting you with disappointing comments and useless verbiage. It seemed things were done to send a subliminal message. The Sunday School, would have a birthday drive; each month they would celebrate who ever had a birthday. They would receive a dime from all the adults in Sunday School. Each person would stand in front of the church, and everyone would march around and give their token. It never failed that when my birthday month came around, only one or two people would participate. And yes, I always participated.

While Pastor Brown was ill, my father became acting pastor. One night in bible class while he was teaching, Wayne, my oldest son was siting with a member of the church's son.

Wayne had some candy and the son wanted some. Well Wayne

refused to share his candy with the child. The child got upset and I supposed started to cry. The mother of the child slapped Wayne. It was loud enough that it stopped the teaching for a moment. I was sitting on the second roll from the front. My cousin was sitting next to me, she told me that the sister had slapped my child. Wayne was only six I believe. I said to my cousin, "what that is ashamed, she do not correct her own children." Now I had really matured, because anyone that knows me , knew I would go to bat for my children. There was a gentleman sitting in the front roll, who heard our conversation. He jumps up and ordered my father to have me stand up and apologize before the church. And of course, my father ordered me to stand up and apologize. What was I apologizing for? I did not make a scene, I did not even go back to where Wayne was. I knew , had I gone back there to get Wayne, perhaps I would have showed her how it felt to be slapped. I was dumbfounded. How did this episode turn on me. I did not do anything wrong. I was hurt because my father did not enquire why I needed to apolgize. He did not hear me say anything. He was on the pulpit teaching. Why did I need to be belittled? I stood up, but I just stood there with my mouth open. What was I suppose to say? Different ones in front kept saying that it was ok , just say something. I finally said, " I am sorry that you think I need to apologize." I gathered my children and I left.

After Pastor Brown Passed , the congregation really showed their cloven foot. They pounced on Greg and I like a lion to it's prey. We were scolded and threatened that we were going to be put out of the church, or silenced; meaning we would not be allowed to participate in any church activities.

What did we do?

Well the church wanted us to give them the parsonage, what most people would understand it to be. However this was not an attachment to the church. It was Pastor Browns's home. It was not in the church name, therefore it did not belong to the church. The house was listed under Pastor Brown's previous married name. The only ones that could claim the house was Pastor's nearest kin, which was Greg and I. Greg became the Executive of her estate. The parisioners of the church did not know that Pastor Brown told Greg that he needed to go downtown

and set things in order, before she passed. After finally realizing that the church could not do anything with the house; they decided that they would purchase the house from Greg and me. We were willing to accommodate them, but they offered us two thousand dollars. Needless to say we did not oblige them. From that time on others were told not to talk to us for we were bad apples. I was pregnant with my eighth child and began to have complications. I was in the middle of my seventh month; sitting at the sewing machine , I thought my water had broke. So I called for a friend to come and watch the other children while Andy and I go to the hospital. After I was examined, I was told that I had a serious condition. It was called Placenta Previa. The placenta had dropped and was covering the cervix. It was not my water breaking, but blood gushing. It was explained to me that I would not be able to birth the baby, therefore possible bleeding to death or causing the baby to die trying to pass the placenta. I had never heard of anything such as this. I was apprehensive and did not think it was that serious. My doctor wanted to hospitalize me immediately,but Andy and I refused. My doctor took me aside an explained to me that if I tried to give birth, and somehow I lived, but the baby died , they would prosecute me. I went home, and they sent nurses three times a week to check on me.

I had a friend who was a nurse. She brought me a book. She said that she was not trying to persuade me to go back to the hospital, but she just wanted me to read about the condition, and then make my decision. After I read the book, I then realized that this was serious. So I promised the nurse, that if I started to gush blood again I would come in and do what ever was necessary for my child to have a safe delivery. When the parishioner of the church heard my decision, they said I was faithless and had denied the faith, meaning, I had denied what the church based it's religion on. Now, Andy, my husband said he was ashamed and displeased with me because I waited until he left to go out -of -town to make my decision. First of all I would have made the same decision if he was home. This was my body, it was the welfare of the child, and I was thinking of my other children. Who would care for them If I were to pass. Second of all what husband would go out-of-town with his wife in such condition. Anything could have happened at any moment. Too bad, I was a disgrace to my church and my husband.

But I thank God he gave me the wisdom to make the right choice, regardless of the stigma that was given me.

I had experienced what it was like growing up with out my mother, and as long as I had the power , and God allowed me. I was the only one who was going to rear my children. I was not going to leave that to chance; that perhaps everything would be alright. What if I had lived and the baby died, I still would not have reared my children. The courts would have hung me out to dry. I would never had been able to forgive myself. Ironically, it seemed that the devil wanted to take my life. After I was admitted in the hospital, I was there for about two weeks before I had a cesarean. I was given an Amniocentesis test to check the maturity of the baby and to make sure the baby had no genetic or chromosomal condition. The baby was fine so the surgery was scheduled. During surgery, the doctor said I swallowed fluid. Evidently The doctors thought I had passed, because they claim they could not bring me around. So, they pushed me off into a storage room filled with boxes. I donot know how long I was out; all I remember was I was felling this awful pain. I came to and begin to look around. I thought where am I and what is this pain. Well, the doctor shut off the valve to the catherter , but they left me sitting up with a sheet over my head. I say it was God that had the doctor to sit me up. Normally they lay you down and cover you up. By the doctor sitting me up, the fluid ran down ,but was not able to be released, because the valve was closed . The pain brought me around. I began to holler for help. I heard someone coming down the hall and I screamed as loud as I could. There was a nurse that opened the door, when she saw me she got so scared, that she ran out of the door. A few seconds later an entourage of doctors and nurses burst into the room. I was hollering get this thing off me, and they were mesmerized . The doctor started ordering this and that and giving sharp demands. I said not before you take this off. Little did I know all I had to do is reach down and open the valve. My goodness what a relief!!!! After that I demanded to know why I was in a storage room. The doctor turned pale and apologized over and over." We thought we had lost you," he stated. My next question was well where is my family. They had not contacted them. Then I had to take all kinds of breathing test to see the condition of my lungs.

But all this time noone knew what I was going through. Andy did not

get home from being out-of-town until the next day. But Thanks be to the almighty God; when noone else was there to protect me, He was there. So, no matter, the test or what ever situation you find yourself in. If you put your trust in Jesus, he WILL bring you out. He WILL protect you.

www.ingramcontent.com/pod-product-compliance
Lightning Source LLC
Chambersburg PA
CBHW051226120626
46547CB00013B/1528